IMPLEMENTING STANDARDS
· · · · · · · · · · OF · · · · · · · · · ·
COMPETENCE

Practical Strategies for Industry

Chris Lloyd
and
Amanda Cook

**KOGAN
PAGE**

London • Philadelphia

First published in 1993

Kogan Page Limited
120 Pentonville Road
London N1 9JN

© Chris Lloyd and Amanda Cook, 1993

British Library Cataloguing in Publication Date
A CIP record for this book is available from the British Library.

ISBN 0 7494 0896 0

Typeset by BookEns Ltd, Baldock, Herts.
Printed and bound in Great Britain by Biddles Ltd, Guildford and King's Lynn.

Contents

Acknowledgements

The authors would like to thank all at Transcend Technology for their patience and support during the production of this book. A special thanks goes to Dawn Shepherd for her hard work throughout.

We would like to acknowledge the generosity of SkillSet – the Broadcast, Film and Video Lead Body – for letting us use its standards as examples while still in their draft form.

Introduction

Managers today are being constantly bombarded with new techniques for doing things, new philosophies for reorganising their businesses, new training and development systems for achieving higher outputs. The flak has been especially heavy in the fields of organisational and human resource development over the last 10 to 15 years, thick with 'mould-breaking' contributions from gurus and 'major' new initiatives and exhortations from government.

The main message coming through all this noise is that an organisation, in order to be successful, must develop a strong sense of self-motivation among its employees which leads them to put in the extra effort which will set it apart from its competitors. Whatever the ultimate value of the new managerial, organisational and human resource development philosophies, the idea of competence linked to self-motivation is an important one. New ways of organising and working which stress initiative put a premium on self-motivation.

What all of these approaches also have in common is the time and money it takes to assess their relevance, and then to apply their advice. The movement that has grown up in the UK around the concept of competence in recent years is no exception to this. It has its own jargon, its own literature, its own methodologies and of course its own cottage industry of consultants and academics. It also has a sizeable and steadily growing army of converts in firms and organisations around the country.

These are people who have detected the value that standards of competence can add to the running of their businesses, in amongst all the assumptions and theory and apparent bureaucracy of the national initiative.

This book aims to distil this and provide decision-makers in business with a practical and professional approach to using standards of competence to improve the performance of their people. It sets out to meet managers and policy-makers where they stand – wanting basic information, advice and guidance on the development and implementation of occupational standards which meet the direct needs of their organisation; wanting reassurance that the extensive rethinking and organisational change demanded by the introduction of standards has a worthwhile payback.

The features and benefits of standards of competence are numerous and attractive but realising their full potential through practical implementation is proving more difficult than most organisations, policy-makers and experts were expecting. What we try to do is focus on how the advantages of standards can be maximised, and show how the pitfalls we have encountered in the experiences of organisations on numerous occasions over the last three or four years can be avoided.

So far, the successful implementation of standards, outside of experiments or their limited use with small sections of the workforce, has been rare and difficult to achieve. In this respect, the introduction of competence-based approaches to human resource development and management is no different from that of other complex and dynamic business improvement measures such as total quality management, integrated office systems or learning technologies. Success depends on the right combination of internal and external pressure and support, and the devotion of as much attention to the maintenance of the initiative as to its definition of needs, development and introductory stages.

The emphasis of this book is on the applications of standards of competence in business rather than on competence-based qualifications.

Employer acceptance of the new framework of National and

Scottish Vocational Qualifications (N/SVQ), currently being built on the basis of agreed industry standards, is still in its infancy. It takes decades to achieve change on this scale. Unsurprisingly, we find that businesses are far more interested in the primary benefits of using standards to reshape productivity and help increase profitability than in the potential benefits of linking into an embryonic framework of national qualifications.

WHAT DOES THIS BOOK DO?

The aim of this book is simple. The vocational qualifications system in the UK is undergoing fundamental change based on a new approach to defining the levels of performance expected from people at work. The methods being used to define these performance requirements and then assess people's competence against them are potentially extremely useful to industry. This book explains why they are useful and how to apply them within your own organisation.

Among other things, it

- discusses the competence philosophy;
- reviews the politics and developments surrounding standards;
- shortlists and describes useful planning techniques;
- provides decision-making support frameworks;
- contains off-the-shelf troubleshooting guidelines on the use of the standards-setting methodology;
- puts forward tried and tested structures and procedures for standards-development teams and working groups; and
- indicates the time and resources required to implement competence-based systems for assessment, reward and development.

We do not claim that this book will turn its readers into instant experts, but we do believe that it will improve the quality of their decision-making in this area and save the time and money of managers setting out to understand the relevance and possible applications of standards of competence to their own businesses.

WhƆ IS THIS BOOK FOR?

It has been written with three groups of readers in mind:

- Those who are thinking about standards of competence for their own organisations and want to know more.
- Those who work for firms and organisations that are already involved in setting and implementing standards and want help.
- Those who know that standards are starting to be expected and/or implemented by their customers or competitors and want to know why.

It is not a book for experts or academics.

When we talk to the managers of firms and organisations about competence, what they really want to know – apart from the obvious 'What's in it for us?' – is 'How relevant are the standards underpinning the new National Vocational Qualifications to our business?', 'How are the outcomes of all these different initiatives supposed to work in our organisation?' and 'How do we make it work for us?'

This book will help managers avoid at least some of the pain and expense of the trial-and-error approaches that they would otherwise have to take when answering these questions. It draws on our extensive experience of working with people of all levels across a wide range of occupations and sectors to set standards, design qualifications and help people interpret and get the best value from what is happening nationally.

The book contains many useful action checklists, and we have scoured the materials we have prepared for literally hundreds of workshops in recent years to provide you with several prototype slides and acetates. We have also made every effort to ensure that the information we give is accurate and up to date.

1

The Drive for Competence

Much has been said and written about competence in recent years, most of it leading-edge arguments about methodology. There is nothing inherently wrong in this but the time is now ripe for a more practical, commercial treatment of the subject. Standards theory might be in place but the challenge to the competence movement now is to put its theory into practice. This chapter will introduce the theory of competence but then explain the practicalities of its application in the real market place.

NATIONAL AND SCOTTISH VOCATIONAL QUALIFICATIONS

A new system of qualifications is being put in place in the UK to support the efforts of employers and their employees to raise standards of performance in the workplace and improve the UK's competitive position in domestic and international markets. They are called National Vocational Qualifications and Scottish Vocational Qualifications (NVQs and SVQs).

These qualifications are based on a new approach to describing and assessing people's performance, ie competence. The essence of this approach is that people should be able to demonstrate what they *can do within the workplace*.

COMPETENCE
The ability to perform
activities to the level
expected within
employment.

How 'well' they perform is judged against a set of standards
agreed nationally by their industry and assessed by experienced
members of the industry. It is up to the individual being assessed
to prove his or her own competence against the standards by collecting and presenting evidence of one kind or another of the
way they do their job. Standards are explicit statements of the
practical things people need to be able to do, and the
underpinning knowledge and understanding they need of why
they are doing something and how.

**STANDARDS OF
COMPETENCE MEAN:**
- Better performance at
  work.
- 'Can do' qualifications.
- Self development
  breakthroughs.
- Objective, needs-driven
  assessment.

Characteristics and components of competence

Competence has two main characteristics. First, it should be
demonstrable, based on actual performance requirements in the
day-to-day work environment. In other words, standards of

competence are all about what people can do, not how much they know or how long they have been employed. Second, standards are concerned with the result of an activity (the outcome) rather than with the inputs that were needed to achieve it. Standards are all about the quality of what you do, not how you go about it.

The structure of the standards against which a person's competence is judged is illustrated in Figure 1.1. It is basically very simple but is often the greatest source of confusion for newcomers to the competence approach, mainly because it is cloaked in jargon. This subject is dealt with in some detail in Chapter 3 (Setting Standards) but a brief overview follows here.

An *element of competence* states what the person should be able to do. It is supported by *performance criteria* which describe the most critical aspects of performing the element 'well' in the workplace. Every element has a range statement which describes the varying circumstances with which someone will have to deal while still able to demonstrate competence. A *unit of competence* is a collection of elements representing a work role that is worth recognising. National or Scottish Vocational Qualifications are made up of units. *Setting standards* involves the identification of the competences required in the workplace and the definition of the standards to which people are expected to perform.

Identifying competences

The method used to identify competences is called *functional analysis*. Beginning with a definition of the key purpose of any given occupational area, it provides a technique for breaking this down into constituent functions and for further dividing these into units and elements of competence. The associated performance criteria and range statements are then defined for each element. Each element also has a set of evidence requirements attached to explain what sort of assessment is needed and what evidence is required to meet the standards.

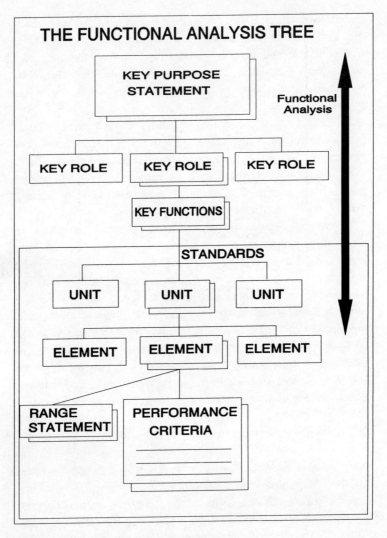

Figure 1.1 *The functional analysis tree*

STANDARDS OF COMPETENCE ARE:

- Statements of what someone should be able to do.
- Statements of how you would judge this.
- Statements of when and where you would expect them to demonstrate their ability.
- Statements of the type of evidence you would need to ensure that their performance is consistent and can be sustained.

The refreshing and most useful thing about standards of competence is that they are derived from a top-down look at what functions are required to support the mission and objectives of a business, an occupation, a profession or an industry. For this reason, the national initiative to establish competence-based qualifications for the workforce has the support of government, the Confederation of British Industry and the Trades Union Congress. It has the full involvement of leading UK Examining and Awarding Bodies (EABs) like Pitmans, City & Guilds, the RSA, BTEC, SCOTVEC, and many professional institutes and institutions, and is quality assured by the National Council for Vocational Qualifications (NCVQ) in England and Wales and the Scottish Vocational Education Council (SCOTVEC). More recently, the government launched the General National Vocational Qualification (GNVQ). This is a competence-based prevocational qualification aimed at boosting the quality of the labour young school leavers can offer employers. While not really a subject for this book, it is a very important development and organisations that recruit heavily in this age bracket will need to be aware of its meaning and implications.

The success of the competence movement to date

The reform of the UK system of vocational qualifications is a very large and ambitious undertaking which, if successful, will influence economic efficiency, occupational status, industrial relations and rewards.

In a relatively short time – since the mid to late 1980s – the initiative has developed considerable momentum and expanded its concerns to encompass the development of standards and design of qualifications for higher and professional-level technical, professional and managerial occupations as well as lower-level ones. Chartered accountants, chartered engineers, personnel managers, trainers and developers, and scientists are all now exploring the development of vocational qualifications frame-- works. The opportunities presented by professional bodies and trade unions to establish firmly standards of competence as a common currency in large numbers of occupational and industrial sectors are just beginning to be realised.

Meanwhile, this UK revolution is starting to be exported to Europe (where Britain is flexing its muscles in the debate on the equivalence and mutual recognition of qualifications within the Community), and to Commonwealth countries like Australia and New Zealand, as well as South Africa.

Nearer to home, one of the main questions currently facing government is how to mobilise the self-interests of these professions and engage them fully in the cause. Around £80 million has been invested in the development of this framework so far, about half of it by the government and the rest by industry. To get a return on this, and achieve the initiative's longer-term aims of providing cost-effective, easy and universal access to assessment and accreditation, there is now the need for two main types of action:

- More work is required from the technical community of competence experts and converts to give a better idea of what opportunities and services are available for the benefit of different types of organisations. This has to include realistic appraisals of the broad scale implications of decisions to implement standards and competence-based assessment systems in circumstances where short-term returns on investment may not accrue.

- As the national competence scene becomes more complex, promoting and delivering increasingly diversified information and services, so more effort must be put into ensuring access to such information and services by first-time and casual enquirers, not just experts. Most organisations are willing to change, at least to some degree, but most are not prepared to take on large amounts of extra work to bring this about. Standards and N/SVQs must be seen to simplify their lives, not add extra complications.

Getting the message through to employers

Already there are early signs of employer frustration with the national competence movement. This is caused not so much by the current profusion of national competence-related initiatives and pronouncements as by the many different, often conflicting, sources of advice and information in this area. As more and more new firms and organisations enter the competence arena, they find that there is no obvious central source of advice or information on the general state of play. One way or another, a lot of public funds and private money has been focused on this area for quite some time; yet, despite the belief of those directly involved in the production of national standards and N/SVQs in the transformational powers of competence, relatively little has been achieved thus far by way of organisational take-up. There are two main reasons for this:

- First, the sheer difficulties have been underestimated – implementing standards in firms and organisations of various kinds is a multi-faceted process which must be understood and worked upon on several fronts. Getting one or two aspects of this task right is not enough.

- Second, the competence movement still has not won the argument – the case for standards needs explaining better and more often to policy-makers, who must be persuaded of the long-term benefits of standards-implementation and of the advantages of formulating long-term strategies of their own to achieve this. The reasons we hear most often from employers for not adopting N/SVQs are that they appear to involve a lot of extra expense for little gain, and that there is too much bureaucracy involved in taking on the formal role of an approved assessment and verification centre within the N/SVQ system.

Government seems to have got this particular message, in this area of its activities at least. Awareness raising and implementation are now emerging as the main components of its funding strategy, with a clear shift taking place from development (an activity for specialists) through dissemination to implementation (something everyone can participate in). These points also apply to industry. Clear guidelines have to be set by decision-makers there as well, if they want to foster the development and successful utilisation of competence-based performance systems which support their medium to long-term objectives.

UNDERSTANDING THE COMPETENCE MOVEMENT

Lead bodies and industry training organisations

At the national level, standards of competence are being set for different industries and occupations by what are called lead bodies, most of which are also industry training organisations (ITOs). These are made up of businesses, employer organisations, professional bodies, trade associations and unions. There are about 160 of them (see Appendix A) and the scale of their activity ranges from that of the Management Charter Initiative (MCI) which has over 100 licensed assessment centres around the UK, to that of the many lead bodies and ITOs which are still at the stage of standards-development or qualifications design. Their job is to identify what has to be done by people within their industry or sector – the competences needed – and then set national standards against which employers think people's performance should be judged (see Figure 1.2).

They also recommend how qualifications can best be built up from modular 'units of competence' to match the current and anticipated performance needs of industry. Two-thirds or so of all lead bodies now have ITO status. Whereas lead bodies are principally concerned with national standards-development and N/SVQ design, ITOs have wider responsibilities for N/SVQ implementation, skills monitoring and ensuring the relevance and adequacy of sectoral training arrangements. Some ITOs have been formed by ex-industry training boards like EnTra, the British Polymer Training Association and CAPITB. Others like the Telecommunications Vocational Standards Council and SkillSet (broadcasting, film and video) have been established as a result of lead body activity. In all of these organisations standards are at the centre of a re-examination of the present and future needs of the industry in terms of personnel performance and qualifications.

The national initiative has now reached the end of a hectic phase of activity during which the lead bodies were formed and began to grow into ITOs. Hundreds of sets of national standards have been laid down and hundreds of new N/SVQs have been put in place. Attention is now turning to how the overall quality and market acceptance of all this work can be raised, and how the structure of the competence movement can be simplified.

Occupational standards councils

Since 1991, lead bodies, ITOs and professional bodies have

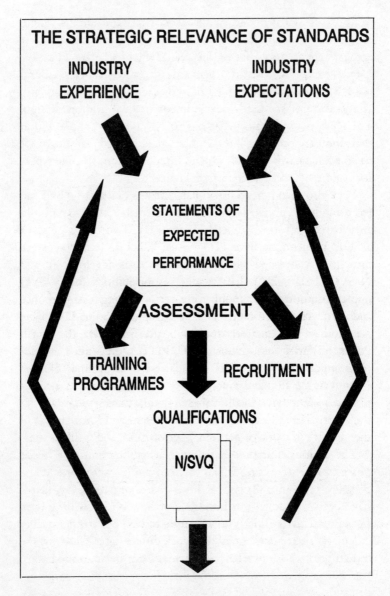

Figure 1.2 *The strategic relevance of standards*

begun to form into groupings called occupational standards councils (OSCs), initially to ensure that common standards can prevail in higher and professional-level areas. At first sight, OSCs look like another layer of unnecessary complication and bureaucracy in an already cluttered national scene. But policy-makers are hoping that the advent of OSCs could have exactly the opposite effect by rationalising communications, the allocation of public funding and the direction of research, development and marketing activities in this area. Only time will tell.

KEY PLAYERS IN THE COMPETENCE MOVEMENT

Lead bodies
Industry training organisations
Occupational standards councils
The Department of Employment
NCVQ and SCOTVEC – the
    accrediting bodies
Awarding bodies
Professional bodies
Trade unions
Employers and trade associations
TECs (Training and Enterprise
    Councils)
LECs (Local Enterprise Companies)

Qualifications and awarding bodies

Individual N/SVQs are offered to candidates by awarding bodies which have made successful proposals on their design, marketing and support to the lead bodies and ITOs responsible for setting particular sets of standards. N/SVQs can be offered by different awarding bodies in the same area. They are awarded when candidates have shown that they can provide enough and the right

sort of evidence to prove that they meet all the performance criteria for all the competences across the stated range of situations.
As Figure 1.3 shows, there are five levels of qualification ranging
from foundation at level 1 to professional at level 5. The
descriptions are taken from the NCVQ Criteria (1991). (See
Appendix C).

Applications of standards

At the same time as all this is happening nationally, increasing
numbers of employers are busy identifying their own competences, matching the results of this against the standards set by
lead bodies, then deciding to what extent they are happy to use
and customise lead body standards as opposed to setting their
own.

STANDARDS CAN BE USED:

- as a basis for job descriptions;
- to identify training needs;
- to develop training programmes;
- as a basis for assessment and reward;
- as benchmarks for development.

What these companies are acknowledging is that standards have
many benefits beyond qualifications. By defining standards of
competence for their workforces which are based on future
requirements and enshrine good practice, employers can develop
a strategic addition to the usual range of business improvement
tools at their disposal.

LEVEL   DESCRIPTION

Level 5   Competence which involves the application of a significant range of fundamental principles and complex techniques across a wide and often unpredictable variety of contexts. Very substantial personal autonomy and often significant responsibility for the work of others and for the allocation of substantial resources feature strongly, as do personal accountabilities for analysis and diagnosis, design, planning, execution and evaluation.

Level 4   Competence in a broad range of complex, technical or professional work activities performed in a wide variety of contexts and with a substantial degree of personal responsibility and autonomy. Responsibility for the work of others and the allocation of resources is often present.

Level 3   Competence in a broad range of varied work activities performed in a wide variety of contexts and most of which are complex and non-routine. There is considerable responsibility and autonomy, and control or guidance of others is often required.

Level 2   Competence in a significant range of varied work activities, performed in a variety of contexts. Some of the activities are complex or non-routine, and there is some individual responsibility or autonomy. Collaboration with others, perhaps through membership of a work group or team, may often be a requirement.

Level 1   Competence in the performance of a range of varied work activities, most of which may be routine and predictable.

Figure 1.3 *Five levels of competence-based qualifications*

THE MAIN BENEFITS OF USING STANDARDS

The processes of developing and implementing standards and competence-based assessment can yield some very important major benefits to employers and employees alike.

Objective performance benchmarks

Standards of competence are designed around the things that need to be done in an organisation. They do not enshrine personalities, job titles or the way things have always been done. Individuals can prove their competence at doing something against the standards whether they are wholly dedicated to a particular role, eg exporting, selling, training using information technology, or merely performing a part of their work role – even though their job title might not acknowledge this contribution. Standards are very specific about the types and breadth of competence that are expected, the criteria against which performance should be judged and the kind of evidence that assessors (see Chapter 5) will need to consider when reaching a judgement. This information is as clear to the people being assessed as it is to their assessors. So there can be no question about what performance is expected, how that will be judged or what evidence will be looked for.

Workplace assessment

Competence is best assessed in the workplace. This actively involves line managers in the development of their people, whose needs are charted against the clearly specified standards. It is in this area that most employers detect the greatest potential gains from shorter communications chains, more devolved authority and opportunities for line-manager development.

26

Clear progression paths

Standards provide employers and employees with a means of identifying career progression targets and paths open to them. They can motivate and stimulate a culture of self-development and open up opportunities to build flexible, transferable skills in the workforce. In this respect, they are part of a general movement away from prescriptive human resource development approaches to more open management systems where the emphasis is on individual self-guided learning and self-motivated progression.

Quality assurance

Clearly specified standards backed by competence-based assessment systems enable employers to extend their quality initiatives to the development and performance of the workforce. Competence-based assessment is effectively a quality system for people which offers important synergies with mainstream total quality and quality standards approaches.

National recognition

Both employers and employees can gain from the fact that N/SVQs are slowly beginning to give recognition to competence-based standards for different occupations. Improved performance and higher levels of professionalism result in better business results and increased motivation.

PLUGGING IT ALL TOGETHER IN THE WORKPLACE

The big problem facing firms and organisations which see gains in taking the standards of competence path is understanding how

27

it can be made to happen in the workplace. There are plenty of organisations which have taken on board the standards set by specific lead bodies, and applied them in limited areas of their workforces. There are fewer examples of companies which are attempting a top-to-bottom implementation of competence-based assessment or reward programmes. This is usually because, in larger organisations at least, a competence initiative will have to compete for time and resources with other improvement schemes, each of which will have its champion and assert major benefits for efficiency, productivity or profitability.

Employer and employee perspectives on competence

There is a complementary relationship between the objectives of an organisation and its individual employees and the operation of a competence-based assessment system. The way in which an organisation responds to its market environment also influences the two-way relationship between it and its people. As Figure 1.4 illustrates, organisational culture shapes employee attitudes towards performance, learning and progression while individual attitudes to learning, competence and personal aspirations form the organisation's human resource. Standards of competence and competence-based assessment operate at the heart of this rela-tionship and have important consequences for quality assurance, training effectiveness, self-development culture, human resource management and the impact the organisation can make in its competitive market environment and that the individual can make in the labour market.

Common learning experience of early users

This book is a synthesis of the experiences, good and bad, of a wide range of companies which are currently working, or have worked, with standards. The learning experiences of these

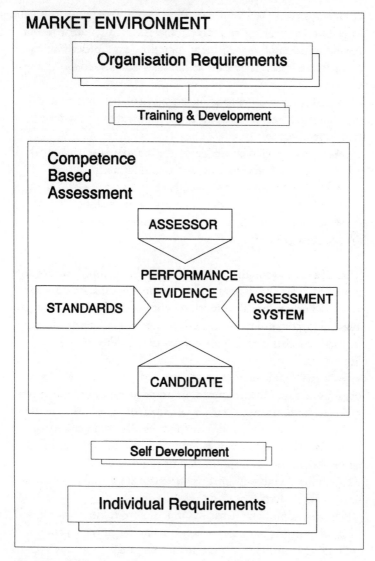

Figure 1.4 *Maximising human potential through standards*

companies will be vital to the next wave of firms and organisations seeking to convert their current human resource development and management practices and procedures to a competence base. They can be summarised as follows:

- Most new users have underestimated the time required to master the philosophy and technicalities of standards of competence.
- A thorough knowledge of the standards-setting work of the lead bodies is essential to successful progress.
- Standards of competence have the potential for a much wider application than in accreditation alone.
- Business needs, rather than standards or qualifications, must come first.

This chapter has sought to demonstrate that competence is much more than simply an array of skills or the capacity to acquire areas of knowledge. The development of attributes such as self-awareness, personal qualities and the understanding of one's role in the ever-changing circumstances of working life are just as important.

Properly implemented, standards of competence can help organisations eliminate waste in their labour utilisation, and motivate and improve their people's performance. Mistake them for a stand-alone solution, fail to invest the time and effort to understand the philosophy and techniques behind them, and they will wreak havoc. The application of standards within any organisation must be viewed in the context of its structure, attitudes, needs and objectives.

The take-up of standards has much more to do with the willingness of organisations to change, to invest in their people and to innovate in their management. Organisational take-up of standards will depend upon the degree to which their design meets user needs in relation to productivity, costs and learning. Standards are value-adding – they do not replace good management nor can they operate independently of strategy. We have learned that standards can galvanise the management of change in organisations but that they alone cannot carry the day. Organisations which view standards of competence and associated assessment systems in the context of their overall human resource development and management activities will be the ones most likely to realise the economies of scale they have the potential to achieve. In the meantime, important assertions about the efficiency and effectiveness benefits of standards-implementation need to be tested rigorously and their results carefully disseminated if the interests of employers and employees alike are to be captured.

2

Relating to the Outside World: Untangling the 'Competence Movement'

Any organisation which thinks it can quickly get abreast of the activities and outputs of the so-called competence movement is deluding itself. As has already been discussed, there is no single information point, hundreds of organisations are involved and the status and quality of the standards and qualifications produced by these organisations vary enormously.

BEFORE YOU START

Before you commit resources to the task of undertaking a detailed assessment of what is happening and how it relates to your organisation's interests and circumstances you need three things:

- a clear idea of what you are looking for;
- a clear and reliable system for storing, collating and comparing the information you gather; and
- well-informed staff.

As soon as you have identified your standards team, it will probably be a good idea to put together two or three intensive briefing sessions for them, run by outside experts. Figure 2.1 overviews the contents that you should expect these sessions to cover.

NATIONAL TARGETS

The staff involved in exploring the potential of standards of competence for your organisation need to have a sound appreciation of the philosophy, principles, techniques and processes involved in the design, development and implementation of standards. This book is a good starting point, but to maximise the effectiveness of your staff and the reliability of their judgements, they need exposure to hands-on use of the functional analysis technique, issues relating to assessment systems design and practice, and the implications of implementing standards of competence for industries and organisations.

LIFE TIME LEARNING

- By 1996, all employees should take part in training or development activities.
- By 1996, 50 per cent of the workforce aiming for NVQs or units towards them.
- By 2000, 50 per cent of the workforce qualified to at least NVQ 3 (or equivalent).
- By 1996, 50 per cent of medium to large organisations to be 'Investors in People'.

The competence movement is a complex one, driven by government policy, supported by a plethora of intermediary organisations, involving relatively large numbers of employers. At its heart is a set of government-inspired national education and training targets for 'Lifetime Learning'. What these targets have in common is the implicit and large assumption that

Functional analysis	Assessment	Implementation
The competence-based approach	*The national framework*	*Implementation options planning*
• Concept of competence	• Awarding bodies	*The development process*
• History and structure of the competence movement – national targets, funding structures, key players, new qualifications structure, applications of competence	• Accrediting bodies	*Consultation, testing and piloting*
	• Quality control	
	• Training and Development Lead Body assessor units	*Introduction and maintenance*
Standards and qualifications	*The assessment process*	*Evaluation*
• How standards work	• Purposes and processes of assessment	
• How N/SVQs are designed	• Who is the assessor?	*Updates and reviews*
Using functional analysis to identify competence	– options, roles, skills	
• Processes and procedures	• What is evidence?	
• Key purpose statements, key roles, units and elements of competence	– types of evidence	
	– systems implications	
Setting standards	• Role of managers in assessment	
• Processes and formats		
• Performance criteria, range statements, knowledge and understanding	• Costs of assessment	
Managing standards development	• Planning new assessment systems	
• Approaches and phases		
• Working arrangements		
– group structures and controls, pitfalls, assessability, resources and commitment, jargon, timescales		
Applications of standards		
• Reward schemes, training needs analysis		

Figure 2.1 *Outline of contents from typical briefing sessions on standards of competence*

employers are going to be prepared to shoulder a rising burden of costs associated with the implementation of N/SVQs in the workplace. Together, these targets provide the rationale for the overall initiative and for a very large number of contracts – between the Department of Employment and the accrediting bodies, the lead bodies, industry training organisations, occupational standards councils and the training and enterprise councils – which drive the initiative along. These contracts are what makes the competence movement tick. The Department of Employment is a natural point of call, therefore, for anyone setting out to get acquainted with what is happening nationally (see Appendix B).

SCOPING YOUR INTERESTS

An organisation which has responded well to the fundamentals of the competence approach and wants to know a lot more should scope its interests carefully at the outset. How extensive an exercise this is will depend upon how large, complex and clear the organisation is about itself.

Start scoping your requirements by answering these questions:

- Where does our organisation want to be in five years' time?
- What are the human resource and organisational development implications of this?
- Which parts of our workforce are most critical to the achievement of this and why?
- What benefits are we seeking from the use of standards of competence and N/SVQs in pursuit of our objectives?

The answers to these questions will have a direct effect not only on your information gathering but also upon your internal prioritisation and planning, should you eventually choose to take standards of competence on board. At this early stage they will help you focus your thoughts, narrow down the information sources you need to investigate, and provide a framework for deciding if and how to pursue the matter further.

When you finally start gathering information, your approach ought to be systematic, otherwise you will soon get lost. Categorising, versioning and indexing the information you collect is essential, as is a contacts database. Very often you will come across more than one version of a set of national standards because lead body and ITO document control is not always all it should be. Most standards models go through several stages of evolution, sometimes involving dramatic changes in content and presentation and always involving references to the work of other lead bodies, especially the cross-sectoral ones. Some lead bodies will supply you with their national standards for free, others like the MCI and the Information Technology Industry Lead Body will charge for them.

TYPICAL PRODUCTION PATHS

In this respect, the important thing to be aware of is the classic production path that the lead bodies are locked into (which will be more or less similar to the one your organisation would embark upon – see box).

Not all lead bodies are at the same stage of development, the various events on this production path don't always occur in the same order, and sometimes some of them do not occur at all! At the time of writing, some – primarily those about to tackle standards-development for higher and professional-level occupations – are in the early stages of their work. Others areas like retailing, construction, management and telecommunications have almost completed it. If your areas of interest happen to coincide with those occupational areas where standards-development progress is still in its infancy, then you have to decide whether to wait until they are developed or develop your own. Alternatively, you could get involved in the work of one of the lead bodies as a consultation point or test site, or as a direct participant in its decision-making. Again, in either case, your decision should rest

---

Typical production path for standards and N/SVQs

- Occupational mapping
- Formalisation lead body/ITO
- Functional mapping
- Standards-drafting
- Industry consultation and modification
- Agreement of national standards
- Assessment system design and testing
- Piloting of standards and assessment systems
- Design of qualifications framework
- Appraisal of awarding body proposals
- Submission of qualifications framework and awarding body recommendations to NCVQ or SCOTVEC

---

upon what your organisation is trying to achieve and why. It need not be an all or nothing decision. There is no reason why you should not develop standards where others do not exist and then gradually shift over to using the nationally agreed ones when they come out of the pipeline.

The process of developing standards of competence by this sequential route has much in common with classic software production paths. Whereas user requirements analysis takes pride of place in the annals of successful software production, implementation is at least as vital to the production of standards of competence. Lead bodies and organisations which view it as a discrete component of the production cycle to which the others relate only sequentially do so at great risk to the enormous amount of effort, commitment and resources the whole process takes.

No amount of tail-end quality control or retrospective market testing can alter this fact. Make sure the lead bodies you are interested in have properly consulted with industry and that the work they have produced stands a good chance of acceptance and adoption in the industry before you go too far down the road with them. And make sure that your own organisation recognises the importance of a needs-driven approach to designing and implementing human resource innovations. If it does not, you might end up with a solution which everyone likes but which stands no chance of implementation.

3

Setting Standards:
Functional Analysis and
Project Approaches

This and the following chapter take you from a ground-floor understanding of the products of a standards-setting exercise, through the methods and controls needed to derive those products, to a position where you can feel confident that you appreciate the scope and requirements of any standards-setting project that you may wish to undertake.

In highlighting stumbling blocks which are common in the field, we either suggest how these can be resolved or provide you with sufficient understanding of the problems to make decisions which are suited to your own particular circumstances.

A few words of warning before you continue:

- Successful standards-setting, by an organisation or a lead body, depends more on project management and involving the right sort of people than technical expertise.
- There are no such things as right answers in standards-setting, only sensible and justifiable judgements. Functional analysis is an approach, not a formula for producing the right result when information is fed in. Developing

standards relies on a thorough understanding of the competence philosophy and the objectives of your project.

CHALLENGES TO STANDARDS-SETTERS

With these two caveats in mind, the greatest challenges to standards-setting are as follows:

- *Misjudging the magnitude of the task.* There are few ways of cutting time consumption. Meetings are invaluable but, regardless of how good the person in the chair, they are almost always protracted because standards challenge traditions. Arranging meetings between managers, supervisors, and other workers with full diaries, causes time delays. Issues have to be debated, they will not go unchallenged for long.
- *Fighting misconceptions.* The greatest enemy is hostility to the project, normally born of misunderstanding. Time invested in educating all participants is time saved sorting out potentially acrimonious disputes later on.
- *Gaining credibility.* Without the ownership of those who will be using the standards in your organisation, the credibility of your work will be low. Standards of competence are supposed to be industry led. This goes for standards set by individual organisations as well as those developed by lead bodies. Where there is poor employer representation on a lead body, the standards-development process usually fails to reflect adequately the needs and commitment of the market place; its products lose credibility as a result. Likewise, in an organisation, the people who are going to be asked to perform their jobs to the standards are the ones who should be most involved in developing them.
- *Fighting other battles.* Standards are not a panacea. They are a valuable tool for recruitment and selection, but they will never replace interviews. They can reveal illogical work

organisation and provide a sound rationale for change, beneficial to all parties, but with the wrong kind of management involvement they can also reinforce prejudices and put various interest groups on the defensive. Standards are often seen as a threat to accepted training structures and programmes, to those whose career paths have been hitherto linked to institution membership, to existing grading schemes and work divisions. They threaten the status quo; they are 'subversive'. Standards-setting projects are beset with political problems of this kind. Dealing with these issues and taking care to communicate with people eat up a huge amount of time and energy which must be accounted for in your project plan.

WHY CONTINUE?

Given these dread warnings, why on earth would you still want to continue? The answer is that well-managed standards-setting is a means of achieving organisational regeneration, personal growth and problem resolution even if, perversely, the final products are never used. The main benefits of this process are summarised below.

- *Information exchange.* Working group leaders and members from a project in car manufacturing explained to us how much they felt they had gained in terms of understanding the requirements of other members of the standards-setting team from different occupational areas and how this had enhanced their capacity to improve their work environment and organisation.
- *Rationalisation and unification.* The standards-setting programme of SkillSet - the lead body for broadcast, film and video - has enabled the industry to agree on common functions across all occupations for the first time. This has united the industry around its requirements to set standards and, through its industry training organisation,

to review the training arrangements to support their attainment.

SO WHAT ARE STANDARDS?

Quite simply, standards are a tool for assessment. They are a set of statements which, if proved true under working conditions, mean that an individual is meeting an expected level and type of performance. They are a way of describing

- what someone ought to be able to do;
- how you would judge they had done it well;
- under what circumstances they would have to demonstrate their ability; and
- the types of evidence needed to ensure they could do it consistently and on the basis of sound understanding, rather than by luck.

The constituent parts of a standard all have jargon terms but on the page the make-up of a standard is *not* that complicated. Despite this, jargon is one of the greatest barriers to standards take-up. Figure 3.1 demonstrates a common format used to define standards of competence.

THE SHOCK OF OUTCOMES

What makes these performance standards different from a training specification or a British Standards Institute (BSI) standard is that they are based on what can be glibly termed as 'outcomes'. We use the term 'glibly' because the concept of an outcome is an extremely tricky one, and causes much argument and confusion in the national standards-setting arena, in spite of the fact that it is at the foundation of the competence philosophy.

The concept of outcomes and the method for deriving standards stating them will be examined in detail later on in this chapter.

UNIT TITLE:	Provides a description of a group of elements (suitable to stand alone on the NCVQ database)		
ELEMENT TITLE:	States what a person should be able to do		

EVIDENCE REQUIREMENTS AND ASSESSMENT GUIDANCE

Performance Criteria	PERFORMANCE EVIDENCE		
		Direct Performance Evidence	Product Evidence
(Evaluative statements, which describe an outcome of performing the element, which if proved true of the person will attest to their competence)		*Details the situations required by the performance criteria against which the achievement of the standards must be demonstrated by performance evidence. Also details how much evidence is needed, ie frequency of performance across the range.*	*Details tangible outcomes/products which could be used as evidence and how much is needed.*

Range Statements	KNOWLEDGE EVIDENCE		
		Underpinning Knowledge	Circumstantial Knowledge
(List the different circumstances in the workplace which the person will have to encounter and still prove their competence)		*Details knowledge of* *a) methods* *b) principles* *c) theories* *which are constant to competent performance*	*Details knowledge which allows candidates to make decisions concerning, and adapt to, varying circumstances:* *a) information (eg legislation)* *b) culture (eg house/production styles, responsibility structures).*

ASSESSMENT GUIDANCE

	Generally details the assessment methods, and how different 'bundles' of evidence compare (this might appear as a separate document).		

Figure 3.1 A standard in a typical format

Essentially, standards are interested in what a person can 'do', ie the achievement of the overall aim of several activities (the outcome) rather than the process they went through to produce it (the inputs required).

An example of this might be in the performance of health and safety risk assessments. In the final analysis you need to be sure that an individual is capable of taking health and safety precautions. The process by which the employee achieves this is to identify the hazards, assess the risks and identify the precautions they will need to take. Similarly, when producing a design for a television production a designer will have to go through the process of meeting and phoning the director and producer, exchanging initial ideas and even sketches, giving advice, suggesting possibilities, taking advice from others and scoping the size and cost of the production. All of these inputs will have to occur on one or several occasions, over an extended period of time. The overall outcome might be that the individual can elicit and agree a design brief.

Getting a firm grasp on this concept is fundamental to successful standards-setting. In our experience it can take quite a while for the penny to drop: up to three successive working group sessions in some instances. Some people never grasp the concept. Thinking in terms of outcomes is like asking people to think upside down; to pinpoint the ultimate aim of a set of activities or to concentrate on what finally resulted rather than all the things that had to be done to get there (such as what came first, second and third).

Misunderstanding outcomes is one of the major hindrances to standards-development projects and a cause of considerable frustration to newcomers. It is also the cause of most distress to first time recipients of standards.

HOW TO READ A STANDARD

Standards always look insubstantial to the people they are aimed at, all the more so where they have been expecting them to be a training tool or job specification in their own right. They can look disappointing or even misleading because it is usually anticipated that they will be the final word on how something should be done. However, they *do not* tell people *how* to do things. They are statements which, if proved true, can assure you that someone has done something well. This is their true purpose.

What makes standards so apparently confusing and threatening to trainers and those interested in training issues is that all the wealth of experience and expertise which was essential to creating them is hidden behind their apparently simple statements.

Standards are like a jigsaw. It is only by understanding how the various parts interrelate that you will see the entire picture. Only once this idea is grasped can their full contents be extrapolated.

THE PRODUCTS OF STANDARDS-DEVELOPMENT

To make their standards more user-friendly producers have developed information packs to accompany them. These have evolved along with the methodology to provide more explanation on their use. The trend has caught on to such an extent that the Department of Employment is currently formalising requirements for such guidance. For individual firms and organisations, it is likely that an information package will contain a suite of components as demonstrated in Figure 3.2.

The standards

The standards themselves comprise functional map, units, elements, performance criteria and range statements. It is likely that the evidence requirements will be shown on the same page as the standards, as demonstrated in Figure 3.1.

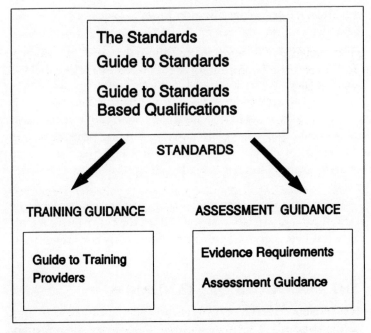

Figure 3.2 *Information support required for standards implementation*

Guide to the standards

This is a booklet designed to make the standards clearer to users, explain the concepts behind standards and explode the jargon. It usually contains the following:

- glossary of terms used in the elements and performance criteria;
- description of occupational areas covered;
- description of the standards-development methods and people involved;
- a statement of the potential uses of the standards within the occupational area; and
- any other information needed to make the standards more assessable to readers.

46

Guide to qualifications (if applicable)

This should put forward the qualifications which are available for the particular occupational area covered by the standards. It will explain:

- how they were developed;
- what levels in the N/SVQ framework they correspond to;
- how people can get the qualifications; and
- the qualification titles, and units required to meet them (including units from other lead body standards, where necessary).

Evidence requirements

As mentioned earlier, these might well appear on the same page as the standards. They state what *sort* of evidence is required, be it direct performance or knowledge evidence to prove competence in all the circumstances required by the range statements. They also detail the *actual* evidence required, eg a tangible outcome, like a report, or knowledge of certain methods.

Assessment guidance

This document is aimed at the assessor of the standards and should give general information on:

- the nature of the assessment process;
- the N/SVQ approach to assessment; and
- sources of evidence.

It should also provide unit-by-unit guidance on assessment including:

- the relative strengths and weaknesses of different types of evidence for particular purposes and their equivalents;
- the period of time over which assessment should occur;
- rules for defining when sufficient evidence has been obtained; and
- identification of assessment-critical situations.

Guidance for training providers

This is to help training providers develop training which can meet the requirements of the standards.

However user-friendly in its design, this amount of information can be a turn-off to busy people. Nonetheless, you will have to be familiar with this information in order to analyse the standards developed by other organisations – particularly the lead bodies – should you wish to use them. Be prepared to design similar documents to assist the use of your own standards. You can keep them short and tailor them to your own needs and industry jargon. Explanatory literature is an essential tool to counteract the greatest enemy of standards-implementation – misunderstanding. There is no guarantee, however, that people will read your materials, no matter how well written, informative or succinct. When marketing or taking standards to a wider public, personal contact must lead the way.

Having examined the products of standards-setting, you now know what might be expected of your project. To give you a few numbers: the entire set of standards for the lead body for accountancy up to level 4 have been formatted into 135 pages; the Heating and Ventilation Contractors Association formatted 34 pages of standards at NCVQ level 2. Be prepared for the creation of a substantial standards-document and supporting information, unless the scope of your project really is very limited. In the next section we will go back to basics, answering the question 'How are the standards themselves derived?'

DERIVING STANDARDS BY FUNCTIONAL ANALYSIS

Functional analysis is the method adopted by the Department of Employment in order to ensure that the standards of competence being developed by lead bodies are comparable in format and consistently outcome based. Functional analysis is, however, only an approach and does not guarantee results. Outcomes are a concept, not a certainty.

In essence, functional analysis is more a questioning and focusing device than a methodology. It relies as much on people's abilities to grasp the philosophy of competence, and facilitators' abilities to control group inputs, as it does on any step-by-step process. It is a technique for arranging a hierarchy of functions so that you can best describe an occupational area from its overall purpose down to the individual contributions needed for the fulfilment of that purpose. It is not an equation, so failure to understand the need to analyse the area in this way will result in failure to do the breakdown properly. Functional analysis does not necessarily provide the right answers, only the information needed to judge what the answer might be.

The three tenets of functional analysis

Functional analysis is a top-down approach

Standards of competence are based on the ability to perform to the level expected within the workplace. In order to identify this in outcome terms, the standards-setter needs to understand the overall aims or purpose of the workplace itself, to which all other outcomes contribute.

Only by starting at the top, with the 'key purpose statement' for occupations across your entire organisation can you begin to organise a functional breakdown in a helpful and efficient way. cient way.

Once this is identified, all you do to pursue the breakdown is ask 'what other outcomes have to be achieved to fulfil the key purpose statement?' Most standards-setters use the question 'what has to be done to achieve the key purpose statement?', but this can tempt people back to thinking about the process of how things happened – what came first, second and third.

This question is repeated until the outcomes identified are of a nature that is achievable by one individual. Functional analysis, therefore, is used to develop a tree of hierarchies, much like a family tree, as far down as the units and elements. When you get this far you have what is called the functional map. A standard is comprised of an individual element of competence, its performance criteria, range statement and evidence requirements. Of these, only the element is derived through functional analysis. Thus, functional analysis should be seen as a focusing device which serves to transport you to the point where the standards-setting begins.

Functional analysis must identify discrete functions

Functional analysis is so called because it identifies functions separately from their job context.

They are transferable between the job contexts; for example, in the broadcast, film and video industry, film laboratory technicians, projectionists and camera assistants all have to receive and log, handle, transport and package film materials. They perform these functions for slightly different reasons and in different contexts but the function is the same. The notion of transferability is at the heart of the competence philosophy as it applies nationally. The idea is that functions should be acknowledged as important in their own right, independently of their contexts. This approach is held to be in the interests of all organisations because it avoids the need to repeat an element of competence in more than one unit and thereby the need to assess someone's competence in an element several times.

Functional analysis must maintain its wording format

Functional analysis has a particular format of sentence building which should be followed. The structure of statements at all levels down to and including the elements should be Verb–Object–Condition (see Figure 4.6, p. 74). This format is essential to ensuring that:

- you identify outcomes;
- consistency is maintained across all standards-setting projects (this is essential for comparability both within your project and when you come to analyse standards developed elsewhere); and
- you state clearly what is actually being done and that the hierarchy is a logical fulfilment of each level above.

It is precisely this wording discipline which makes standards the assessment tool that they are. In breaking the wording rules, standards-setters defeat their own purpose, no matter how sensible or self-evident their own methods of describing the elements and performance criteria are.

Functional analysis is not a science

Bearing the above tenets in mind, it should be clear to you by now that functional analysis is more of a 'black art' than a scientific methodology. The greatest controls on the process are as follows:

- The past experience of your facilitators; their familiarity with concepts of competence and the pitfalls of the analysis process.
- Participants' ability to switch-on to, and be supportive of, the new perspective of outcomes.
- Thorough briefings and refresher courses.

STANDARDS-SETTING IN ORGANISATIONS

Project phases

Standards-setting traditionally goes through the phases shown in Figure 3.3. It is a mistake, however, to see the process as linear because to be successful standards-setting has to be an iterative process.

First, there is the presence of several formalised testing and consultation phases. These can be multiplied according to the timescale and sensitivities of the project. They are essential for a lead body because if the standards are to represent the requirements of an entire industry they have to have been made available for comment to a good sample of all the sectors and sub-sectors, sizes of business, and regions likely to be affected in that industry. Consultation has to be used because the development of the standards themselves can only involve a limited number of participants.

Second, the work is subject to a multitude of revisions during any one phase and between different phases. Up to the very last moment, standards are never written in stone, and nor should they be. During development, their robustness comes from constantly rethinking problems and rearranging units and elements until the best solution is found. Even when they have been completed, they will still need to be updated as the workplace changes, to maintain their best-practice position.

The functional map will need revising and modifying during most stages of the process as its hierarchy is refined by further work and thinking. Similarly, while writing performance criteria, groups will reveal knowledge and understanding which becomes part of the evidence requirements. Developing range statements is fundamental both to clarifying the scope of the elements of competence in stage 3 (consolidating units and elements) and to the successful completion of stage 6 (identifying evidence requirements). Your work in stage 4 (writing performance criteria

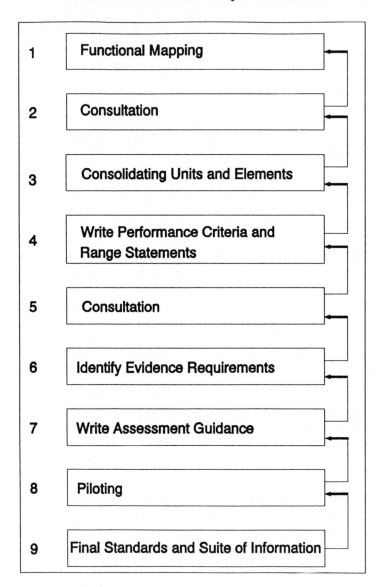

Figure 3.3 *Project phases*

and range statements) may well require the rethinking of your original range statements.

Standards projects are by their very nature in a constant state of flux. Just as all the constituent parts of the standards themselves are interlinked, so are the various stages of their development. Any project co-ordinator must accept this as par for the course and be able to distinguish the aims of each stage while being flexible enough to make changes in past work where necessary.

Project products and their uses

Figure 3.4 illustrates the aims of each stage of the process and the uses for the products of each phase. Functional mapping might even be split into two stages within your organisation's planning, as a very rough map of the largest functions may well be vital to your scoping exercise, prior to any commitment to a more concerted effort. All of these phases should be supplemented by events within your organisation to include, educate and update people who are not directly involved in the work but eventually will be using the standards. Be careful not to let information about the project and its contents leak into the organisation without sufficient explanation. People very rarely take the word 'draft' as it is intended.

HOW TO APPROACH A STANDARDS PROJECT

Different projects and consultancies go about the collection of the information for standards-setting in a variety of ways. However, the general methods remain the same. They are combined much as in any other project you will have been involved in, according to time, money and labour availability.

The emphasis placed on the use of consultants can vary widely. Your decision on their input can have major implications for the way that your project integrates with other initiatives in your organisation and the ways in which you see standards benefiting your organisational structure or culture.

There tend to be two main approaches to using consultants. Your project can be people-led or consultancy-led. In general, we recommend the people-led approach because, although there are advantages and disadvantages to both, this option pays dividends if standards are planned to be used as a serious tool for organisational change and human resource development. Consultants still have an important role to play in the process but the emphasis is set squarely on the leadership and participation of the organisation's own employees. These are the people who will have to make the system work in the long run, and no amount of consultancy input can prepare them for this responsibility if they are two stages removed from the design and development process.

Other factors inevitably come into play when you are deciding on your approach; will the organisation release participants in the project?; will management have confidence in a project which does not call on consultancy expertise?; will the management have confidence in a project which heavily involves consultants?; what is the budget? A brief rundown of the advantages and disadvantages of both approaches may shed some light on the decision.

The people-led approach

Advantages

- Produces a core of employees who understand and can spread the competence message to their colleagues.
- Working group involvement eventually leads to high commitment from participants. This can make a few good representatives from the teams into excellent ambassadors for the work during its development and marketing.
- Any change apparently imposed from above, or conceived in isolation, will cause automatic suspicion. If an organisation plans to use standards in connection with pay or rewards, and they are too strongly associated with

Stage	Aims	Uses
1 Functional Mapping	• To develop an overview of all the functions in an occupational area or organisation • To begin the breakdown to enable standards to be developed (often, but not necessarily, as far as draft units and elements).	• To identify which functions within an organisation are exclusive to it, ie will need to be prioritised for development because no one else will do them. • To identify which functions have already been developed by lead bodies (eg management) and, therefore, will not need development, or be a lower priority needing careful consideration of existing work prior to development. • To identify working group structures for standards-development based on the functional areas in the map. • To examine the scope and priorities of any potential standards-setting exercise. • To demonstrate and explain standards philosophy.
2 Consultation	• To gain acceptance for, and to identify improvements to, the initial hierarchy.	• To ensure no functions are missing. • To ensure the language is understandable to practitioners. • To confirm or improve the hierarchy of functions. • To promote the first stages of the work and explain the philosophy behind it.
3 Consolidating Units and Elements	• To review the functional map to develop a stable structure of units and elements ready for standards setting.	• The structure against which performance criteria and range statements will be set.
4 Writing Performance Criteria and Range Statements	• To produce a set of standards capable of assessment.	• The basis for any assessment uses of the standards: performance criteria provide the evaluative statements against which the person is assessed, the range statements delimit or detail the circumstances under which the element and performance criteria should be performed and evidence collected.

5	Consultation	• To gain acceptance for, and identify improvements to, the entire standards.	• To ensure no units or elements are missing. • To ensure units and elements are accessible in their current packages and with the draft range statements. • To ensure the language is understandable to practitioners. • To ensure the performance criteria and range statements are complete and accurate. • To gain comments from a wider audience not previously involved.
6	Identifying Evidence Requirements	• To provide a set of evidence specifications.	• A set of specifications which will make the standards assessable in a universally applicable manner.
7	Writing Assessment Guidance	• Explain how to meet the evidence requirements.	• To ensure assessors understand all the requirements of assessing competence. • To ensure the performance criteria and range statements are complete and accurate.
8	Piloting	• To confirm, or improve, the assessibility of the standards. • To confirm, or improve, the guidance to assessors.	• To ensure competences are assessable in the workplace. • To accustom people to workplace assessment and the philosophies/methods of assessment of competences.
9	Final Standards and Suite of Information		• Incorporate any feedback and changes from the above phases. • Contains all necessary supplementary information to make standards user-friendly.

Figure 3.4 *Aims and applications of the phases of standards setting*

management demands, their benefits in terms of providing a platform for objective appraisals and stimulating self-motivated learning will be lost.

Disadvantages

- Working group structures are inevitably time intensive. Even a meeting once a month can be hard to co-ordinate in full diaries, leading to time slippage. This can be solved by intensive, residential courses.
- Working groups are resource intensive and costs can be high, given the level of personnel required.
- Certain participants will take time to win over and can be destructive in the process. Feelings may run high, but it is worth trying to keep the majority on board.

The consultancy-led approach

Advantages

- Can be faster than working group structures. However, consultants still need workshop support.
- Less resource intensive for an organisation in terms of drafting time, document control, people involvement.
- An impartial eye can be essential to functional analysis in areas which have been traditionally viewed as having particular divisions. Without this, functional analysis can be wrongly used to reinforce existing organisational processes.

Disadvantages

- Ownership: standards imposed from elsewhere have few supporters with a vested interest or commitment to encourage their uptake.
- With the best will in the world, consultants do not have the in-depth knowledge of the occupational area. If they

are incapable of understanding the nuances of an occupation, or interpret functions wrongly, it can cause friction and frustration all round.

- Consultants often provide a 'formula' functional analysis which meets the needs of NCVQ and SCOTVEC, but not necessarily the precise needs of your industry or organisation. If you want to use standards primarily as a tool within your organisation, you must find a consultancy that is willing to meet your needs first, and yet is capable of keeping you on track when your instincts, or those of your managers, buck against the competence philosophy.
- A project in which the majority of the work is conducted by a consultant may well achieve technical acceptance but the content can be weak if the consultant has not been able to have access to, or elicit, the right information. Workforces who have had minimal input to the standards will not understand them.

We firmly believe the benefits of standards accrue from breaking the 'pain barrier' within your own organisation: doing it and owning it yourselves. It is not wise or economic, however, to do without consultants at all. They do have the past experience, the understanding of the philosophy, the links with the outside world and the external view of your organisation which will prevent you from going completely wrong and (re)writing an analysis which enshrines the way things have always been done. The onus is on you to point out to consultants where suggestions cannot work in your environment, but accept that you will for a long time be thinking in a mindset that is totally contrary to competence; what might be anathema early in the project seems very logical later on. Successful standards-setting comes with educated and dedicated working groups combined with judicious use of consultancy expertise. The ideal standards-setter is a practitioner with at least two years experience of writing standards in the field. The working group methods described in this book will not create such an animal overnight, but they can start your colleagues off on the right path.

4

Setting Standards: Methods and Technical Control

Regardless of your approach, the methods of standards-setting are pretty universal. The key to a successful project is to mix, adjust and tailor them to your particular needs and occupational area. For example, a questionnaire is not going to be completed readily by people who work outside on a dirty, windy and wet building site. It's all a matter of common sense and sensitivity to the types of people and workplaces encountered. Figure 4.1 illustrates the most common methods used against each phase and the types of aids that can be employed. Terms like 'key representative' are explained later in the chapter.

WORKING GROUP STRUCTURES AND CONTROLS

Working group structures

The main challenge to any standards-setting exercise lies in the management of a substantial flow of information and people. In

STAGE	METHODS	AIDS
1 Functional mapping	• Desk research • Working group/key representative meetings • Questionnaire surveys • Workshops • Document circulation • Interviews	• Troubleshooting sheets • Jargon explanations • Functional analysis briefings • Structured workshop questions
2 Consultation	• Expertise/consultation workshops • Questionnaire surveys • Document circulation • Interviews	• Briefing meetings • Explanatory literature • Helplines
3 Consolidating units and elements	• Working group meetings • Key representative meetings • Questionnaire surveys • Expertise workshops • Document circulation • Interviews	• Troubleshooting sheets • Jargon explanations • Functional analysis briefings • Structured workshop questions • Helplines
4 Writing performance criteria	• Working group meetings • Expertise/consultation workshops • Questionnaire surveys • Document circulation	• Troubleshooting sheets • Examples
5 Consultation	• Expertise/consultation workshops • Questionnaire surveys • Document circulation • Interviews	• Briefing meetings • Explanatory literature • Helplines

Figure 4.1 *Methods and aids in the standards-setting process*

an environment where drafts are continually changing and the meat of the project is created through discourse and debate, effective communications and controls must be central to all your project-management techniques. The major steps to a robust management set-up involve:

- Effective central co-ordination.
- Regular meetings of working groups to avoid isolation.
- Rigorous methodological control.
- Rigorous document control.
- Time invested in educating participants.

Figure 4.2 demonstrates a structure for standards projects involving several working parties, which has been tried and tested across a range of organisations and work settings.

The co-ordinator

In this model there is always one co-ordinator in a virtually full-time post who has a vision of the overall project. It is essential that this person becomes thoroughly familiar with the competence philosophy and the process of standards-setting so that he or she can safeguard the vision of your organisation and properly deploy expertise from external consultancies. To be effective, the co-ordinator must have a strategic input into the objectives of your organisation. Many projects fall down because the central co-ordinator has neither the position nor the vision and understanding to push the project through. This means being prepared to meet deadlines yet being flexible enough to make pragmatic decisions over time slippage where quality might be sacrificed. In organisations where the co-ordinator is denied access to the organisation's strategic planning, or is hamstrung by layers of management hierarchy, projects flounder for lack of direction.

The co-ordinator will be responsible for:

- chairing and fixing agendas for the key representatives' meetings;

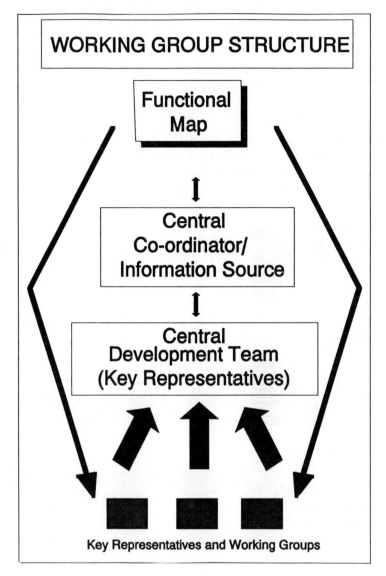

Figure 4.2 *Working group structures and controls*

- monitoring and maintaining the methodological and technical integrity of work in association with the consultants;
- co-ordinating working group meetings;
- co-authoring explanatory literature;
- representing the project to all levels of the organisation in briefings and meetings; and
- setting and monitoring the work plans and resource allocations in conjunction with the consultants.

The organisation of working groups

The model presented in Figure 4.2 relies upon the existence of a functional map. Each working group is given responsibility for a section of the functional map and is populated by practitioners working in, or having responsibility for, that area. This method of work division is illustrated in Figure 4.3.

Key Representatives

Each of the working groups is led by a key representative, who acts as chair and representative of the group's interests in any discussions concerning the overall project. Their main responsibilities are to:

- chair and facilitate meetings;
- control the drafting of the standards documents;
- attend key representatives' meetings;
- represent the project during consultations and implementation; and
- act as the contact between the co-ordinator, the consultant and the working group.

To fulfil these duties the key representative needs:

- A firm understanding, or willingness to grasp, the competence philosophy;

64

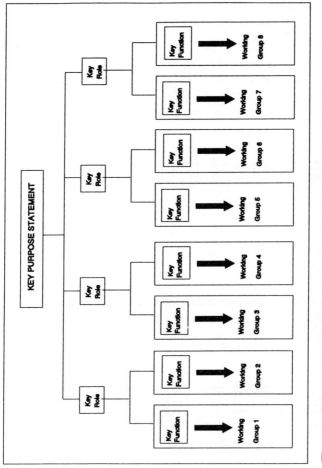

Figure 4.3 *Working group organisation based on a functional map*

- strong chairing skills;
- clear time commitment for meetings and work on documents outside meetings; and
- experience of a wide range of occupations within the functional area.

Standards are best developed when the key representative takes an active interest in the project's success out of genuine commitment rather than pressure from superiors.

The key representatives should meet on a regular basis to discuss the progress of the overall project. The interchange of tips, methods and findings at these meetings is essential to avoid the isolation of any one working group. It is also valuable in ensuring that the working groups adhere to the accepted philosophies and do not blaze a trail of their own. The meetings should also serve to cover any problems of overlap between the groups and inform them of progress outside the immediate project which impacts on their work. Working groups are always eager to see the work of other groups and projects to pick up tips for dealing with their own problem areas.

The feeling that no one else is in the same boat, and the frustrations this breeds, frequently dishearten people. Regular meetings of the key representatives can avoid this by creating a sense of project identity.

Setting up a working group

A working group should be composed of about seven members. This normally means identifying 14 different candidates, who will attend an initial briefing. Real opponents, or those with not enough time, can be weeded out at this early stage. The profile of the group should be representative of the variety of functions within the area likely to make up the entire functional area and also representative of a variety of levels of performance. Group members should *not* all be high level representatives. Inputs should be from practitioners with an overview of the occupation at a higher level and those who actually perform the functions identified.

The group must be up-to-date with current developments in their field. Standards should always be forward looking – set with an eye to the future rather than the past. Otherwise, there is a danger that they will merely enshrine past working practices, not best practice for the future.

Working group members should be picked with care. One member inclined to be obnoxious, awkward, extrovert or opinionated at the expense of other contributors can seriously impede progress made – and annoy the rest of the group. Those with particular hobby-horses should also be avoided, unless they can sacrifice the continued voicing of their own views to the detriment of group progress.

Working groups containing one person with a particularly pedantic frame of mind, quick temper or bombastic manner can make the entire standards project an extremely unpleasant experience. The discord created seriously taints the perceived benefits of the standards themselves.

Having said this, any working group will experience argument, frustration and disillusionment during the course of the project, and this should be pointed out from the outset. Members should be prepared in an initial briefing for the realities of working in groups where answers are not obvious and gaining consensus at each stage is essential but sometimes fraught with difficulties.

The qualities listed below are important in putting together any group, but frankly no one can predict group dynamics and common sense must again come into play in both your selection and any subsequent handling of problem groups or individuals. In summary, group members should exhibit:

- the ability to grasp new competence philosophy;
- expertise in an occupation relevant to the functional area;
- the ability to work constructively in a group situation; and
- time commitment.

Document control

Document control covers the following areas:

- Draft controls and working group notes.
- Methodological advice.
- Access to information.

Draft controls and working group notes

This apparently insignificant area can be the cause of havoc within standards projects because all the painful arguments have to be committed to the working group's latest draft. If the group does not document its meetings in sufficient detail, information is lost. Acrimonious disputes can rear their ugly heads time and time again if decisions are left continually unrecorded or members believe that their input has been lost. Groups can quite literally be working from different drafts. It is no exaggeration to say that lack of discipline in this simple area can waste a significant amount of time. The key representative, co-ordinator and consultant must all be up to date with the drafting status of the group's work.

Methodological advice

All advice on drafts from the consultants to the working groups should be in writing within a formal feedback mechanism as advice given in the context of a working group can be hard to pin down. Within this mechanism it is important to have timescales understood from the outset. Groups that ask for feedback in the morning for a meeting in the afternoon are unlikely to receive a good-quality reply. Consultants should make sure that a working group does not attend meeting after meeting without formal responses to their work. Again, these are commonsense issues, but in busy workplaces, where the project comes secondary to the group's everyday responsibilities, they can be fudged to the detriment of quality and goodwill.

A copy of the written feedback should be forwarded by the

consultant to the key representative and the co-ordinator. This is essential to ensure (a) that the advice is consistent among groups and, perhaps, different consultants and (b) that methodological advice has been given even where it has not been accepted by the group. There have been instances where a key representative has been informed of serious methodological problems within the functional analysis but has withheld it from the group because the information ran contrary to that representative's perception of the occupational area.

Access to information

It is inevitable that if information is leaked to the rest of the organisation, without an accompanying explanation of competence and why standards look the way they do, damage will be done. No standards are sent out 'naked' to the unsuspecting public, this should apply even more to drafts.

The difficulty with draft documents is that, even though they have 'draft' stamped all over them, readers still find them hard to disbelieve. Untold chaos and blind panic can be caused by draft documents getting into uninformed hands when unsupported by all the knowledge which has got the document to that status. Working groups can run with part of the model requiring amendment for some time until a solution is found; the group knows where the model is unsatisfactory, but someone else might not. This point is laboured, because it appears simple but can be the foundation for prolonged animosity and huge time slippage in repairing the damage caused.

A complementary problem is that of who you allow to speak to whom. Without taking on the role of 'Big Brother' the co-ordinator must make it very clear just who represents the project, especially in a large organisation. Some working group members never quite pick up the concept, or interpret competence in their own fashion, and send out completely wrong messages. The co-ordinator inherits the political confusion.

Lastly it is essential that the consultant be kept aware of organisational meetings, decisions and literature which impact on the work. If you choose to keep a consultant uninformed, your decision will make them less efficient in your cause.

EXPLAINING FUNCTIONAL ANALYSIS TO A WORKING GROUP

The explanation of functional analysis which follows will be required by your groups in stages 1 (functional mapping) and 3 (consolidating units and elements).

The suggested briefing session is included in Figure 2.1 on p. 34. This briefing has been tried and tested to make the right impact on working groups. Its emphasis is always realistic, pointing out the vital importance of understanding the new perspective of outcomes and outlining the potential frustrations of standards-setting in a group context.

Functional mapping

Before you reach the stage of instructing the standards-setting working groups you will already have had to create a functional map to demonstrate all the functions required in your organisation.

The working group for this early stage should be made up of people who can represent all the potential functions within your organisation, although more than seven or eight members can be unwieldy. Quite possibly they will be the type of people that you would consider as key representatives later. The functional mapping stage is a start point to be refined by consultation. It will not be right first time, hence the need for the consolidation of units and elements in stage 3, but it is worth the investment of time and energy to get a sound foundation for your working groups to build upon.

A functional map is a breakdown either as far as draft units and elements, or as far as is deemed necessary to decide on the areas where working groups will take over.

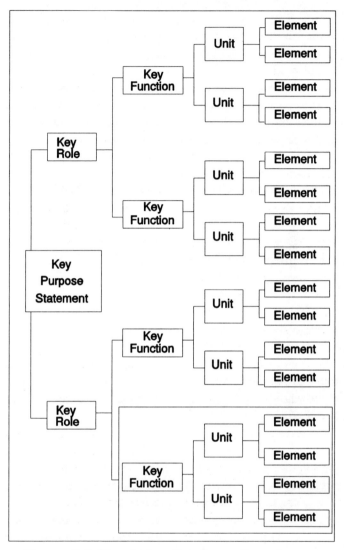

Figure 4.4 *Classic functional map format*

Figure 4.4 shows the classic functional map. An area, like the one boxed, will be taken on by the working group which will either work with it or revise it. Usually, there will be several levels of breakdown between the key roles and any units. The number of levels will probably differ along each branch of the tree. In other words, maps can look a lot more ragged, as shown in Figure 4.5 A functional map ultimately provides the 'workings out' or the justification for the structure of your standards.

THE FUNDAMENTALS OF FUNCTIONAL ANALYSIS

The key purpose statement

The key purpose statement is the focus for the entire breakdown of functions. It should state in outcome terms the reason for your organisation's existence; what you are here to do, or achieve. It is likened to a mission statement, but you do not need the flowery claims that these often contain such as 'world class customer satisfaction'. This evaluative statement means nothing until the whole of your workforce is actually meeting the very standards that will be laid down by your project. You are not here to create customer satisfaction (a phrase that one working group called 'the prostitute statement') or profit alone – that is taking the idea of an outcome too far and could be claimed by most organisations. The aim of the key purpose statement is to provide a focus for your work which makes the aim of your organisation clear to the practitioner and the lay person. For the purposes of the project, keep it simple. If you want to do a cosmetic job on it later for outside eyes, do so, but during the project don't expend too much anguish or energy on it, because it can become a battlefield in itself for little purpose. The key purpose statement is the first statement to be written in the Verb – Object – Condition format.

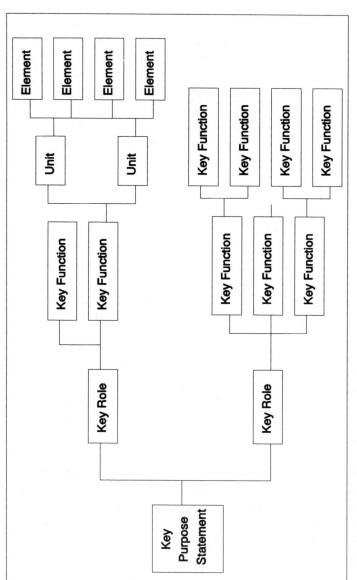

Figure 4.5 *A more realistic functional map*

Original Sector	Active verb/phrase	Object (what)	Conditions/ Context
Broadcast, film and video	create, provide and disseminate	radio, film, television and electronic productions	for general and specific audiences

Figure 4.6 *The Verb–Object–Condition format*

Some tips on the development of key purpose statements

- Always make your groups brainstorm in a Verb – Object – Condition format on their flipcharts, as shown in Figure 4.6.
- Gather all the suggestions on one chart and discuss the objections to each word or phrase used in turn until a sentence is chosen by elimination. This smacks of the old adage 'a camel is a horse invented by committee' but it normally prompts agreement or a sometimes brilliant alternative out of the blue.

In summary, a key purpose statement is:

- a point of focus;
- written in the Verb – Object – Condition format;
- not the political be-all and end-all.

Key roles and further functions

Key roles (see Figure 4.7) are the next level of breakdown from the key purpose statement and together they should lead to the fulfilment of that statement, in the way that all functions in the tree will have to from now on. Many consultancies in this field have stopped calling them key roles, preferring instead to call them the first level of breakdown. They then number all the levels of disaggregation tier 2, tier 3 etc.

The danger with key roles is to think in terms of the process, ie what comes first, second, etc. Many maps will follow this pattern but functions are not strictly time dependent. Key roles can be a very satisfying level of disaggregation and are worth spending time on because the logic of the analysis really starts to take shape from this level onwards.

In all of the analysis stages from now on, be prepared to accept that a function you originally thought of as being at one level may turn out to be merely a subset of another level you identify

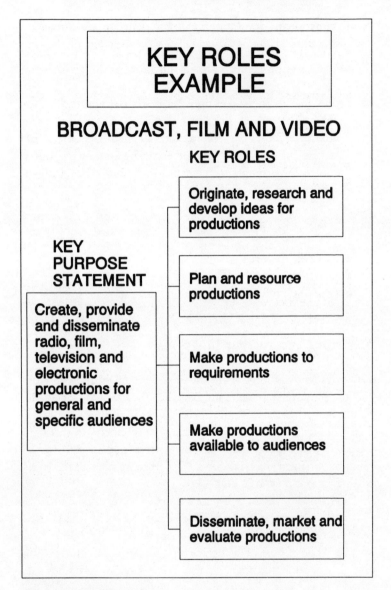

Figure 4.7 *Key roles*

later. Functional analysis consists of moving up and down the hierarchy until all the levels are a logical fulfilment of the ones above.

In summary, key roles and functions:

- are written in the Verb – Object – Condition format;
- must add up to the statement of the level above;
- are subject to continual review and reshuffling;
- can be prefaced by the statement 'the person should be able to . . .'

Elements and units

The elements are the final stage of the functional analysis. They are a statement of what one individual should be able to achieve, even if that achievement will involve working with others or in a team.

The units are more of a convenience for standards-setting in the competence scene than a legitimate part of the analysis. The unit is the currency of National Vocational Qualifications. It is the module that appears on the NCVQ database and makes up the qualifications. It is a description of a grouping of elements which can be recognised, as the NCVQ criteria state, as having 'meaning and independent value' in employment (see Figure 4.8). Although the functional map shows elements after units, in the process of analysis a unit is not so easy to define, because it merely helps to package elements in the way that has most validity in your workplace. The unit should be large enough to make it worthwhile for you to accredit someone with its achievement and award someone a certificate for. This is the reason why it is necessary to have the consolidation stage 3. Functional mapping cannot go into all the debates needed to establish the unit/element packages.

During stage 3, your working groups should not be thinking about levels in their analysis, just what has to be done at whatever

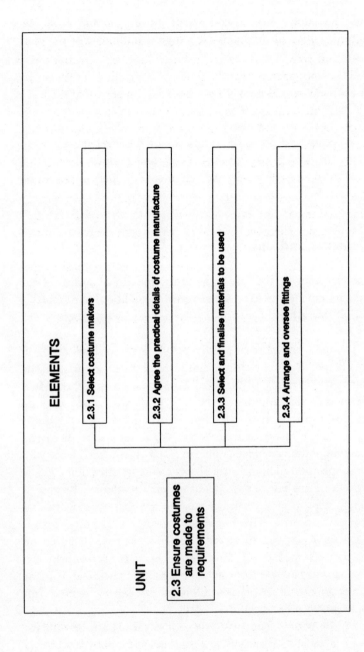

Figure 4.8 *Units and elements*

level. As they move into stages 4 (writing criteria and statements), 5 (consultation) and 6 (identifying evidence requirements), however, and start discussing the circumstances of performance, it will become apparent that the functions identified in the map are just a template which does not reflect the complexity of the levels or different contexts of performance needed. It is then that the map is revisited and new parallel units are developed, based on one unit which acts as a template for these others performed under a different range of circumstances and often at a different level. These parallel units should have a slightly different unit title, and it is likely that the elements, performance criteria, range statements and evidence requirements – especially in terms of knowledge and understanding – will experience readjustments or additions to reflect the distinguishing characteristics of the new unit. Parallel units are developed after the functional analysis has been performed (see Figure 4.9).

Some tips on the development of units and elements

Figure 4.10 illustrates two basic ideas which can aid the group to identify units and elements.

In summary, units of competence are:

- written in the Verb – Object – Condition format;
- a group of elements of meaning and independent value in employment;
- worthy of separate accreditation;
- templates of functions from which parallel units can be created;
- achievable by an individual.

And elements are:

- the last level of functional analysis;
- written in the Verb – Object – Condition format;
- achievable by an individual;
- supported by performance criteria, range statements and evidence requirements and, therefore, assessable.

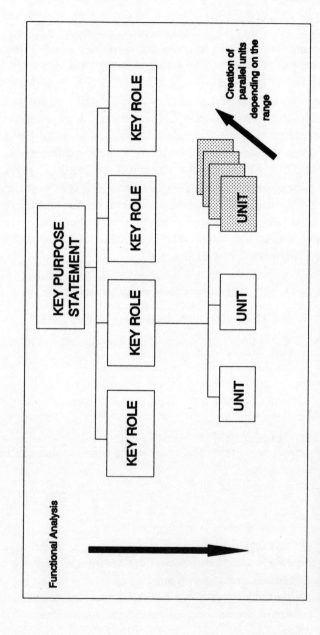

Figure 4.9 *Functional analysis and creating parallel units*

METHOD	HOW TO PROGRESS
Listing the process	When analysing a unit for its elements, it might help if you list what has to happen in order for the outcome to be achieved. But always go back and ask yourself what the outcomes of each of these processes or tasks are. You might end up grouping several into one. A numbering system will help you to do this.
The 'includes' list	When breaking down a function, keep notes on all of the information used to describe its content and applicability, eg draft range statements identified and what the new element contains. This will help you to remember the original element. It is surprising how easily this is forgotten from meeting to meeting.

Figure 4.10 *Working group methods*

WHERE MOST WORKING GROUPS GO WRONG

A major drawback of functional analysis is that it appears to be very language driven. This is to some extent true; the hierarchy must make sense in terms of plain English. A danger of the approach, however, is that groups become too absorbed in arguments over single words or phrases. Groups will ask consultants to draw up lists of useful and banned words. In the end, it is not the words themselves which are inherently good or bad but the thought that goes behind them. For example, the word 'identify' in a functional analysis may be a sign that the map is very time orientated, or formula ridden at the expense of the actual requirements of the organisation. This might be so if every first element of every unit began with 'identify'. The identification may only be a task which allows you to 'do' the next element within the correct parameters, and is the range for the next element. Yet in another map it may be just as acceptable to have a unit or element using the word, if that is valid in the workplace. It is the thoughts behind the words that are important. Warn your groups that if they find themselves dwelling too long on one or two words, they should move on, and return later to re-examine the function.

Figure 4.11 illustrates a number of classic mistakes that standards-setting groups make. Working groups also have a tendency to settle for a less-exacting way of thinking if the disciplines of functional analysis are allowed to slacken. Figure 4.12 demonstrates the 'easier' routes working groups are tempted to take and why they should avoid them.

WHERE FUNCTIONAL ANALYSIS USUALLY GOES WRONG

Troubleshooting functional analysis to element level

The following are a few questions which working groups should ask themselves during meetings to ensure they follow the basics of functional analysis. It can be reproduced as a troubleshooting guide.

Language: Are all the key role, key function, unit and element statements written in the format of Verb – Object – Condition?

When words or phrases with which you are familiar are rewritten in this format it will help you to decide whether they are valid units, elements or even performance criteria. It also helps to clarify

WHAT TO FORGET	WHY
1 Jobs and job titles	(a) Never approach functional analysis by listing job titles and trying to find commonalities. Job titles differ immensely and there are thousands of them. People do slightly different jobs and perform activities in different orders. You will never agree to the content of a unit if you think in terms of your jobs (see point 4).
	(b) Jobs are built up of tasks performed in certain orders; functional analysis acknowledges outcomes achieved regardless, initially, of methods of getting there or timescales. This is where functional analysis is of benefit, because it will not match the structure of your organisation as perceived through jobs – instead, it rationalises and breaks down existing barriers. People never agree on the time order or content of jobs.
2 Levels	The initial functional map is not concerned with levels – only with what needs to be done at whatever level. Some functions inevitably will be performed at three or four different levels, eg managing resources. This is sorted out when consolidating the units and elements in stage 3 or even later. During the functional mapping, all you need is a template of functions performed. The creation of parallel units of a different level or context happens later.
3 Training and education needs	Standards are not a training programme, nor are they intended for trainees. They describe the outcomes achieved by a competent practitioner not a student. If you think in terms of students, you will lower the standards and retain the wrong sort of information in the performance criteria.
4 Timescales	(a) A function is the same no matter where it is performed. Writing a report before the end of a project and writing one at the end is still the same function, not a different one.
	(b) Don't think in terms of doing things first, second or third. Functional analysis groups different activities in terms of the overall aim of those activities, not their order of performance.

Figure 4.11 *Common mindsets: what working groups should forget*

ERROR	WORKING GROUP JUSTIFICATION	REASON FOR ERROR
Using accepted organisational/ jargon phrases or initiative titles eg 'continuous maintenance' or 'staff development'.	We all know what it means.	(a) You don't. People have different understand-ings, even in the same company, of jargon and especially of new initiatives. (b) The jargon alone does not give any identifica-tion of the outcomes and there may be many different functions hidden within it. (c) New initiatives may not be functions in them-selves but part of other functions.
Not following the verb – object – condition format.	We all know what we mean.	(a) You will forget by the next meeting. (b) You cannot fulfil the hierarchy if one level is not worded properly.
Not keeping a full record of decisions made.	Saves time.	(a) Loses time when you can't recall the logic of your own decisions.

Figure 4.12 *False easy routes*

whether they are functions at all, and whether your working group really performs that function. It is too easy to use phrases like 'staff dvelopment' without examining functions within them.

Prefaces: Are the key role, key function, unit and element state-ments written in such a way that you could preface them with the statement 'The person should be able to . . .'?

Forbidden words: Do any of the key role, key function, unit or element statements begin with the words 'know', 'understand', 'use', 'operate' or 'utilise'?

If they do, ask the question: 'What does this knowledge, understanding or ability to use equipment enable someone to do?' Functional analysis is a description of the functions that have to be performed within an area, sector or industry. Knowing or understanding theories, procedures or information which might help you to do something, or knowing how to use equipment that will enable you to do something, has no part in the functional analysis at this stage. It is more likely that this will be transformed into performance criteria, range statements, or the evidence specifications for an element.

Outcomes or processes: Do any of the key role, key functions or unit statements begin with the words 'measure', 'check' or 'review'?

If so, ask the question: 'What is the reason for measuring, checking or reviewing?' Functional analysis concentrates on the results of an activity rather than the tasks which have to be done in order to perform that activity. Some statements which could be prefaced by 'the candidate must be able to . . .' are still, in fact, processes.

'Measure', 'check' or 'review' are all processes which have to be carried out in order to ensure that something is the right length, size, or weight or to ensure that something meets specifications.

Evaluative statements: Do the key role, key function, unit or element statements include words like 'quality', or 'correct'?

If they do, remove them. At this stage of the functional analysis, there is no need to state the standard, only what has to be done. The standard will be written within the performance criteria where you will have the opportunity to describe in detail how you would know that something has been done correctly and to the quality expected.

Repetition of elements: Do the same elements appear in several units?

If they do, re-examine your functional analysis. It is likely the analysis is describing tasks or accepted jobs rather than functions. The repeated elements may well form a new unit.

Overall Coherence: Do all the elements, if completed satisfactorily, mean that the unit has been done exactly as you have described it?

Ask this about each layer of the analysis. If you have done all of the key roles, you should have done exactly what you claimed to do in the key purpose statement. If you have completed all the elements within a unit, you should be satisfied that you have done exactly what was asked of you in the unit title.

WHERE FUNCTIONAL MAPS USUALLY GO WRONG

Political functions

Political functions can be found in maps where a particular occupational area is aiming to upgrade its status. Key roles can appear in a functional map because they are a statement of a new and fashionable theory, not because they deserve to be there in a purely functional sense.

This is currently occurring around the promotion or development of company mission statements. This means that a map may end up being linked to a particular management theory and face the danger of being overtaken in years to come. Giving too much emphasis to departments or parts of the workforce which are manoeuvring to gain status in your organisation or puffing up their own importance can seriously disturb the balance of your map.

Quality of analysis

The following are examples of classic mistakes which should help you to review your functional map.

Skills, job and knowledge-based maps

(See Figure 4.13) Obviously exaggerated, working groups who have not understood competence can produce work like this. The major problems can be summarised into three points.

- The key role and units do not describe what is needed to be done or achieved.
- The elements will all become either range statements eg, 1.1, 1.2, 1.3, or knowledge requirements eg 3.2.
- The units are difficult to gauge until the key function is properly defined. We do not know what outcome they are expected to achieve.

Process and time-related maps

The unit shown in Figure 4.14 needs reanalysing. It has been developed to contain what comes first, second etc. It is too detailed in terms of activities, but does not ask what the aims or outcomes are, eg element 1 is done first, but its outcome is to set up storage conditions which will be suitable for a variety of goods appearing in the range. Many of these elements will become either range statements or performance criteria in larger elements. The last elements belong to the completely different functions of 'maintaining equipment' and 'issuing stock'. A possible reanalysis is shown in Figure 4.15.

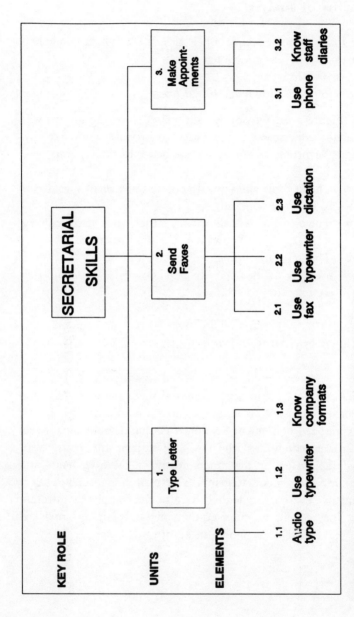

KEY ROLE

SECRETARIAL SKILLS

UNITS

1. Type Letter

2. Send Faxes

3. Make Appointments

ELEMENTS

1.1 Audio type

1.2 Use typewriter

1.3 Know company formats

2.1 Use fax

2.2 Use typewriter

2.3 Use dictation

3.1 Use phone

3.2 Know staff diaries

Figure 4.13 *A skills, job and knowledge based map*

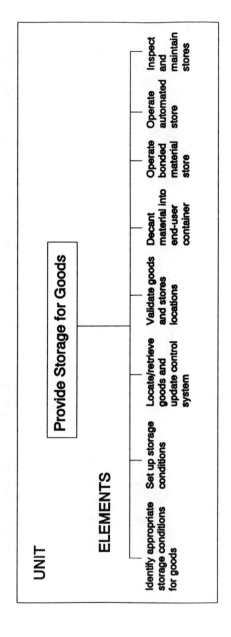

Figure 4.14 *A process and time-related map*

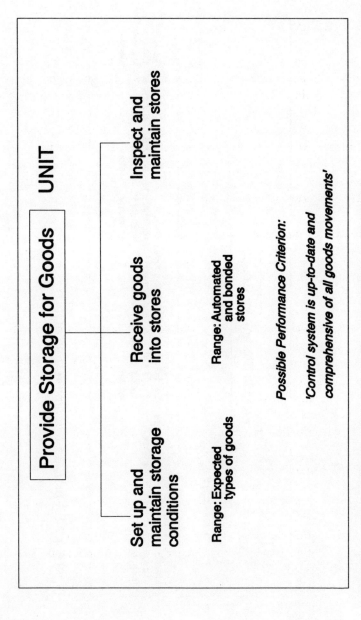

Figure 4.15 *A reanalysis of the process and time-related map*

EXPLAINING PERFORMANCE CRITERIA TO A WORKING GROUP

Once your working groups have got to this stage of the project they will be familiar with the functional analysis techniques. Now it is time to change the emphasis from what has to be done, to how well it is done. The performance criteria are, as the name suggests, at the heart of the assessment tool that is the standard. They are written in a completely different format from the rest of the model and follow the format of outcome – evaluative statement. They are the first evaluative statements the groups will produce.

Some tips on the writing of performance criteria

It is always easier to think in terms of what is done than how well, so don't be afraid to list the process:

1 Write down what has to be done.
2 Go back and ask how would you decide each item on the list was done well.
3 Eliminate those which repeat or those which are too obvious so that those aspects left are the critical ones.
4 Imagine what happens when things go wrong, and the effects of the real workplace atmosphere. Ensure the criteria describe the accepted standard in the workplace.

In summary, performance criteria should:

- be written in the Outcome – Evaluative statement format;
- define the most critical aspects of performance;
- define the level to which the element should be performed;
- address the contingencies and job management aspects of the workplace.

91

PERFORMANCE CRITERIA

ELEMENT: Receive Goods into Stores

PERFORMANCE CRITERIA:

OUTCOME	EVALUATIVE STATEMENT			
Storage of materials	is in designated locations and at safe stacking heights, weights and proximities			
Loss or damage to materials	is reported promptly and accurately			

Figure 4.16 *Performance criteria*

WHERE PERFORMANCE CRITERIA USUALLY GO WRONG

Here are some questions that working groups should ask themselves during meetings to ensure that the performance criteria they develop follow the requirements of NCVQ. We recommend this, even if your organisation decides not to buy into the N/SVQ system and develops its own standards for internal purposes, because it will enhance the value of your standards as a performance-assessment tool.

Language: Are all the performance criteria written in the format Outcome – Evaluative statement?

Standards are not training programmes. Performance criteria do not describe how to do the element stage by stage as if to a novice. Instead they are statements describing the most critical aspects of performance which would allow you to separate a competent performance from an incompetent one. They provide an outcome that the assessor can focus on, and an evaluative statement which, if met, would reveal competent performance.

Forbidden words: Do any of the performance criteria begin with the words 'know', 'understand', 'be aware of' or 'have an appreciation of'?

If they do, ask the question: 'When they are performing the element, what does this knowledge and understanding enable them to do?' Standards are only concerned with knowledge and understanding of theories, procedures or information in so far as they help a person perform to an accepted standard. It is possible for someone to know theories and procedures but never put them into practice.

In the element 'maintain supplies of equipment', a wrongly written performance criterion might be 'Have an appreciation of the organisation's purchasing systems'. This knowledge will allow you to ensure that 'orders are made in sufficient time to prevent stocks running out' (a correct performance criterion). It might also ensure that you request stocks from the right suppliers, or on the correct documentation. These should be the performance criteria, and knowledge of the purchasing systems should be placed in the evidence requirements where it can be investigated to support achievement of the entire element.

Verbs in performance criteria: Do any of the performance criteria contain or end with verbs such as 'is obtained', 'is identified' or 'is checked'?

If they do, ask the question: 'If this is done, how well was it done?' or 'What is the reason for or the result of doing this?' In using functional analysis to reach element level, you are interested in identifying the things that have to be done. In the performance criteria, you now have to describe those critical aspects of the performance which would allow a judgement to be made about whether or not a person had performed the element to the required standard. It is, therefore, no longer so important to know what was done, but to be evaluative about how well it was done.

Sometimes, however, it *is* valid to state what was done. For example, if there are any problems 'the relevant person is informed promptly and solutions are sought and agreed'.

Orders in performance criteria: Do any of the performance criteria begin with instructions such as 'Always check that . . .', 'Demonstrate the ability to . . .' or 'Record the information . . .'?

If they do, ask the question: 'What is the result of doing this and how well is it done?' The performance criteria should not tell the reader how to do the element but provide statements which should be proved true about someone's performance.

Meaningless words: Do any of the performance criteria contain the words 'correct', 'right', 'proper' or 'appropriate'?

If they do, ask the question: 'What is correct in this case?' or 'Appropriate to what?' By themselves, words like 'correct' or 'appropriate' mean very little. If they are used in the standards, it will be left to the assessor to decide what was correct or appropriate at that time. Try and describe what is meant by appropriate or correct in connection with the particular element you are dealing with. For example, to a makeup artist the 'appropriate skin cleanser' might be the skin cleanser which is 'appropriate to the client's skin type'.

Too many/too few performance criteria: The number of performance criteria may indicate the following:

Too few:
- Is the function worthy of being an element?
- Have you examined all the most critical aspects of performance (see point 'Overall coherence' below)?

Too many:
- Is the function trying to cover too much, should it be more than one element?
- Are all the performance criteria really critical?

Overall coherence: If all the performance criteria were met by someone's performance at work, would you be satisfied that they had done the element well?

The standards are concerned with what really makes the difference to competent performance of the element. They are also interested in the way that someone might approach the element if something goes wrong, or the way they work within their environment and interrelate with other people. All these things are important to show that someone is competent not only at doing something but in performing efficiently within the workplace. Keep coming back to the question, 'Are your performance criteria painting a picture of how you would expect a competent person to perform?'

EXPLAINING RANGE STATEMENTS TO WORKING GROUPS

Range statements are where standards-setting starts becoming difficult. By now, your working groups will have grown very adept at excluding the real world of work from their meetings. But once performance criteria become the subject of debate, so too do real work practices and the real contexts dealt with by range statements. Range statements are where you grasp the nettle, and work out how to apply standards in the workplace.

The subject of range and its relationship to writing evidence requirements and assessment needs has always caused debate in the professional standards-setting community. Range statements detail or limit the circumstances and situations under which evidence needs to be provided. As a result, they influence how transferable the unit will be. Their complexity will affect how much evidence will need to be produced. They raise questions of how willing an occupation is to infer competence in contexts which are similar functionally but not traditionally accepted in an occupational area or draw upon different bodies of knowledge. In accountancy for instance, the function of computing tax might be similar but draw upon different knowledge according to whether the tax is for an individual, sole traders and partnerships, or corporates. It might also be performed by different people within the profession. Range statements are normally split into categories which might include types of equipment, products and services, clients and customers, types of environments or constraints.

In summary, range statements:

- provide a link between standards and workplace practice;
- are a focus for assessment;
- can be updated.

By following the controls explained in this chapter, and keeping a sound eye on the aims and objectives shown in Figure 3.4 (p. 56),

RANGE STATEMENT EXAMPLES

1. ELEMENT: Receive and log materials

   RANGE: Types of material:

   * processed film
   * unprocessed film
   * video tape

2. ELEMENT: Record and store information

   RANGE: Recording methods are both:

   * manual
   * electronic

Figure 4.17 *Range statements*

groups will be on the way to producing standards in unit packages with consolidated elements and accompanying performance criteria. They will also have draft range statements and some evidence requirements.

The group's standards now provide a template of units and elements representing the functions performed by your entire organisation. These standards must now be reviewed to turn them into assessment tools applicable to the entire workforce.

5

Measuring Performance: Assessing Competence in the Workplace

A time comes in all standards projects when you can put off facing the issue of assessment no longer. In this respect, developing standards is like hand-wringing a wet towel. As you work your way from one end, a lot of the water in the towel squeezes down to the other, where some stays until you have wrung out the towel completely.

Over the last few years, the standards-development methodology has undergone a similar experience. As its users have tried to formalise and solve the problems inherent in the earlier work of the lead bodies and versions of functional analysis, so those issues which have proved more difficult to resolve have been pushed into the arena of assessment.

Just when you get to the point where you have a finalised set of standards of which you are rightly proud, packaging and assessing them to meet the needs of your workforce will open up another huge can of worms. The main problem areas are the specification of the range statements and decisions about the contexts in which evidence is to be gathered.

A cornerstone of the competence philosophy underpinning the design of the N/SVQ framework is the principle that competences should be transferable. This has led standards-developers to create units describing functions which are applicable to many different industrial or sectoral contexts. To achieve this level of transferability and so meet one of the main criteria for the approval of N/SVQs by NCVQ and SCOTVEC, developers have had to resort to the production of very bland performance criteria, to the detriment of addressing the real situations and differences of context thrown up in the workplace. The main effect of this has been to force statements relating to specific contexts and work roles into the evidence requirements or even the assessment guidance. In the past, this was because both of these components of a standard were known as 'below the line', ie they were not officially part of the standards and could be treated differently by awarding bodies. Today, evidence requirements are increasingly considered as being part of a standard, while assessment guidance is still 'below the line'.

Either way, the adaptation of these components to meet the needs of particular sectors can be self-defeating. The trend is towards having increasingly bland, generic and apparently transferable standards which are actually assessed in completely different contexts in the workplace. This is a worst-case scenario. As we write (early 1993), methodological guidance in this area is still unclear.

Arguments are still raging about the adequacy of the terms being used in this area (evidence requirements, evidence specifications, assessment specifications etc) and there has been little technical guidance issued by the relevant funding, accrediting and awarding bodies concerning their meaning or how present difficulties are to be resolved. This is a natural consequence of evolving a methodology *after* it has started to be used in anger rather than before. Meanwhile, the practical problems of how to assess standards reliably and cost-effectively still need resolving if employer confidence in the national framework is to build.

An increasing number of N/SVQs are being awarded (around 120,000 by the end of 1992) but case studies of companies which have implemented and costed a complete, internal assessment system are still lacking. Consequently, the two most frequent questions about assessment – 'how much will it cost?' and 'how have other companies done it?' – remain unanswered.

In the absence of examples or guidelines, if you are developing your own standards and have got this far down the standards-development path, you should go on to develop assessment systems which meet your needs. These might well be less rigorous and costly than the quality-assurance measures specified by NCVQ or SCOTVEC. For instance, you might not place the same emphasis on the role of external verifiers. At the same time, it would be advisable to remain more or less in line with national approaches to competence-based assessment. This will make it easier for your organisation and its employees to step into the N/SVQ system, should it wish to do so at some later date. It will also prevent you from making any unintended U-turns such as reverting to assessments of competence wholly by skills test or examination!

HOW THE COMPETENCE-BASED ASSESSMENT MODEL WORKS

The theory of competence-based assessment

We have all been assessed and probably assessed others at some point in our lives, from our first attempt at a width of the swimming pool, to the panic of exams at school, or our driving test. We have come to accept these sorts of assessments as an unquestioned part of everyday life. Every assessment has a form of pass mark. At swimming, it was crossing the full width of the pool without stopping or putting a foot on the bottom. The style or speed of your swimming was not important. The distance involved probably bore no relation to the average pond size likely to attract children to its edge. It was simply the length that was available in the nearest assessment facility, your local baths. Exams at college or school use a percentage pass mark, which is usually referenced in some way to the overall achieve-

101

ments of that year's intake. So the pass mark depends on the qualities of your year group, or even the number of people that a particular institution wants to pass.

Apprenticeship, membership of professional institutions, or registration to practise in professions rely on extensive training courses, examinations, practical tests and time-serving to gain experience. Such mixtures of techniques are used to ensure sufficient recall of the knowledge base required, via exams, experience on the job, or through time-serving. But how do we guarantee a candidate's recall in a topic that didn't occur on the final paper? Or in one which didn't crop up during probation? How do we know to what standards a child should be able to swim? The answer is simple: we don't (see Figure 5.1).

Standards of competence work backwards to arrive at answers to these questions. They start by describing the standards of performance required in the workplace. Once these have been set, they require only that individuals meet these standards in order to be assured that they are competent. This assurance derives from a system whereby the individual has to prove his or her ability to match the standards by producing evidence to support their case:

- there is no specified course or training;
- there is no time limit to the assessment;
- there is no age limit for candidates;
- there is no reference to grading or comparison with other individuals;
- anyone can apply but it is likely that the candidate is, or has been, a practitioner in a workplace or a near-workplace environment.

The main challenge facing competence-based assessment is the same one that faces other accepted techniques. How can the assessments provide assurance that the evidence is sufficient and reliable enough to prove that the standards have been met? Traditionally, other assessment methods have tried to get around problems of reliability by employing various strategies to

EXAM CONSULTANT	SCEPTIC
1. The candidate does all the assessment on one day.	But what if the candidate is unwell/off colour that day? The candidate only proves their ability once, ever? Isn't it unfair if the candidate panics?
2. You pick a few questions perhaps three out of an entire course.	But how do you ensure the candidate wasn't only capable of anwering on the three topics that were picked?
3. The candidate learns all of the theories in a place of learning.	So how do you know they can do the job in the workplace?
4. The exam is written.	Is that relevant to ensuring the candidate can develop an accurate design and convey it to other people?
5. The pass rate is norm-referenced to the success of all the other candidates in the intake.	So there is no single standard?
6. The learning centre decides on all the courses.	So how do you ensure it is relevant to the employer?

Figure 5.1 *An argument for exams?*

maximise the chances of reliability: mixing assessment methods, having examining boards, changing the patterns of exam questions yearly and validating courses. Competence-based assessment is no different in this respect, and at this relatively early stage in its development, experiments are still going on to make sure that the assessment strategies it uses are as efficient as possible.

The assessment framework and quality-assurance mechanisms

How it works

Aware of the need to reinforce the reliability of competence-based assessment, NCVQ has recommended a model for assessment and verification procedures which must be met by every awarding body offering NVQs (an awarding body's key purpose is to 'arrange, maintain, monitor, evaluate and review an assessment, verification and certification system'). Even if your organisation chooses to follow an independent course, it might be wise to emulate a similar assessment and verification structure in order to reassure your workforce of its fairness and to maximise your chances to opt into the national framework should you so wish.

The structure you put in place should allow you to:

- review the competence of your assessors; and
- review the efficacy of your systems.

Figure 5.2 describes how the national system is supposed to work. The candidate, sometimes aided by a mentor, presents his or her evidence to an assessor. The assessor judges the evidence aided by meetings with other assessors to ensure that they are all interpreting the standards correctly and agreeing where evidence might be unsatisfactory. An internal assessor countersigns the judgements of the assessors to ensure consistency. An external verifier samples assessors to ensure the assessments are con-

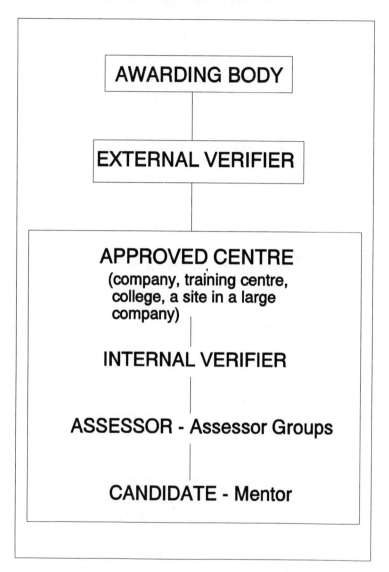

Figure 5.2 *Verification and quality assurance systems*

ducted correctly, following a consistent interpretation of the standards, and also overviews the maintenance of the assessment records. The assessment centre (in an organisation this could be a site, department, or an external college with which you have links) will be approved once it can satisfy the awarding body that it meets criteria concerning facilities and workplace environment, recording systems, assessor training and competence (probably set in accordance with NCVQ criteria and lead body requirements).

An appeals procedure should be agreed whereby the candidate can appeal to the assessor or, if necessary, refer their enquiry to the internal verifier who is in a position to judge the reliability of any assessor's judgements.

Cost implications and reductions

An early cost analysis of a similar system to the one described above revealed that 75 per cent of the money spent on assessment fell into the category of time, travel and subsistence and assessor deliberations over judgements. No research has appeared since to challenge this. The major costs relate to the work of external verifiers. Even organisations not buying into the national system may need external verifiers to ensure assessment consistency if they have several remote sites. The costs of external, and internal, verification may be reduced in a number of ways:

- Ensure your assessment centre is completely set up before verifiers are used. Awarding bodies have lost out by not approving centres vigorously enough in the first place, leading to wasted time and travel.
- Establish and stick to a minimum cost-effective number of candidates at each centre.
- Use local external verifiers or make verifiers share their visits with other centres.
- Be fully prepared for the verifier's visit so you do not waste time.

- Make your standards and evidence requirements as clear as possible to reduce deliberations on how to interpret them.

The assessment process

The process, as depicted in Figure 5.3, is simply one of identification, collection and presentation of evidence. The decision, based on the evidence alone, can only take three forms: competent, not yet competent, or additional evidence required.

Preparation of an assessment plan
The development of an assessment plan, in conjunction with the candidate, the assessor, mentor and manager (if the manager is neither the assessor nor the mentor) is vital to the cost effectiveness of the assessment.

Your plan should identify:

- only those units the candidate should provide evidence for and is likely to achieve from an initial examination of the performance criteria, taking into account present and past responsibilities and roles;
- where training will be required to ensure coverage of the elements and the range;
- evidence which can be used in support of the achievement of several elements, or performance criteria in different elements;
- the timing of workplace assessments to coincide with particular activities apposite to the range or the collection of evidence relevant to the achievement of several elements;
- where another assessor might be needed to cover specialist units or range.

The collection and submission of evidence
Again, this is performed in conjunction with the parties involved in the plan. Evidence is collected together in a portfolio and only

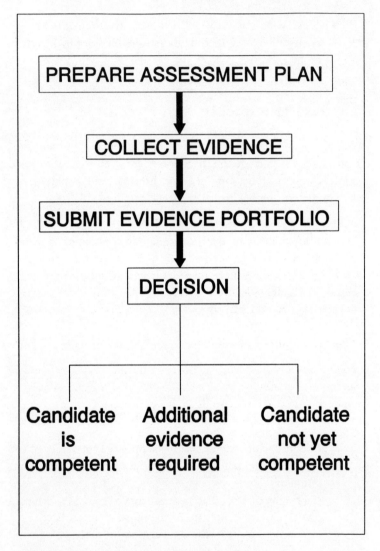

Figure 5.3 *The assessment process*

submitted when it is felt to be sufficient to prove competence in all the elements identified in the plan, across the range.

The decision and sufficiency of evidence
The assessor should consider the evidence provided, ensuring that:

- it meets the specification of the evidence requirements and the assessment guidance concerning coverage of the range and performance criteria;
- it is enough in terms of quantity and quality to prove the person is competent and does meet the standards;
- the evidence was valid for the purposes it was put to and verifiable.

If the evidence does meet these criteria it is judged *sufficient* to allow a confident decision concerning the individual's competence. The decision will be verified as described in Figure 5.2.

The main sources of evidence

Figure 5.4 shows the main categories of evidence sources and the methods that can be used to collect this evidence. The term 'underpinning knowledge' has been another cause of great debate and can be used to describe all knowledge evidence (also called supplementary evidence). In Figure 5.4, it is used to describe that knowledge which ensures constant performance produced as a result of understanding the principles, theories and methods behind the work and procedures. On the page, the evidence requirements might be displayed as shown in Figure 5.5. It is important to note that knowledge evidence is not supplementary to performance evidence, nor is it there merely to provide answers when it is not possible to observe performance, ie 'to fill in the gaps'. It can be gathered at the same time as performance evidence, or at different times, and is complementary to performance evidence.

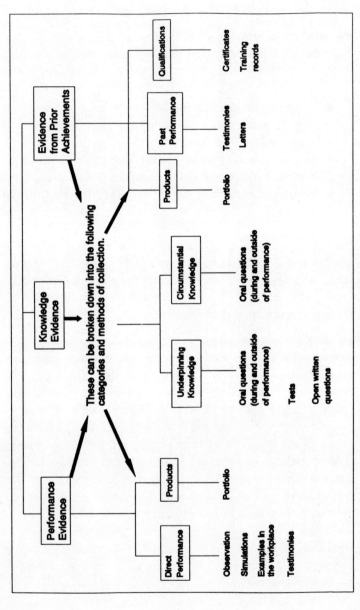

Figure 5.4 Sources and methods of collecting evidence

UNIT TITLE:			
ELEMENT TITLE:			
Performance Criteria	**EVIDENCE REQUIREMENTS AND ASSESSMENT GUIDANCE**		
	PERFORMANCE EVIDENCE		
	Direct Performance Evidence		**Product Evidence**
	Details the situations required by the performance criteria against which the achievement of the standards must be demonstrated by performance evidence. Also details how much evidence is needed, ie frequency of performance across the range.		*Details tangible outcomes/products which could be used as evidence and how much is needed.*
Range Statements	**KNOWLEDGE EVIDENCE**		
	Underpinning Knowledge		**Circumstantial Knowledge**
	Details knowledge of *a) methods* *b) principles* *c) theories* *which are constant to competent performance*		*Details knowledge which allows candidates to make decisions concerning, and adapt to, varying circumstances:* *a) information (eg legislation)* *b) culture (eg house/production styles, responsibility structures).*
	ASSESSMENT GUIDANCE		
	Generally details the assessment methods, and how different 'bundles' of evidence compare (this might appear as a separate document).		

Figure 5.5 *The formatting of evidence requirements and assessment guidance*

Specifying evidence requirements

Mixing assessment techniques

When identifying the evidence requirements and assessment guidance for your standards it is essential to specify a mix of assessment methods. Although the NCVQ criteria state that every element should be assessed by performance evidence, this should (and will need to) be complemented by other methods. Each source and method of evidence collection will have advantages and disadvantages in terms of its sufficiency to prove competence across the range and performance criteria specified by the standards. Depending on the circumstances of collection, therefore, it is valid to establish options in the sources and methods of evidence collection that can be seen as equivalent in sufficiency. In particular, the assessment guidance should state when performance evidence alone will suffice to prove the individual's competence in a particular aspect of the range and when other forms of evidence are more appropriate or considered sufficient to prove competence.

Your decisions concerning the evidence mix can significantly affect both the reliability and costs of evidence collection by:

- ensuring that your assessment does not rely on any one method but instead allows proof of fully rounded competence (too much performance evidence might prove an individual is capable of performing the function but not that they understand it and vice versa);
- allowing for the combination of expensive and cheaper techniques;
- providing options to account for local variations in access to certain methods of evidence collection.

Costs

The cost of any assessment will be in line with whatever is needed to provide sufficient evidence to prove competence to the standards. Any short cuts which compromise this assurance will end up being false economies because the assessment will have no purpose at all, and any money spent will be wasted. It is possible, however, to control the potential costs of assessment through the way in which the evidence requirements are specified:

- Don't overspecify the amount of evidence needed – quantity does not automatically lead to sufficiency.
- Avoid specifying test requirements that will cause substantial outlays.
- Update your requirements where necessary.
- Establish and record precedents where evidence can be used to prove competence over several elements.
- Use the portfolio itself as evidence of record-keeping and information exchange.

Who are the assessors?

After cost, the next questions always asked about assessment are 'who will be the assessors?' and 'how are the assessors themselves assessed?' An assessor can be any one of the following:

- a supervisor;
- a line manager;
- a training officer;
- a college tutor;
- a trainer.

It is likely in a company environment that the assessor will be a line manager or supervisor. They will have to be of at least equal competence to the candidate in the same areas, but obviously it is preferable if they are seen to be more competent because this reinforces their authority and the credibility of the decision they make. It would not be unusual for a candidate to have more than one assessor depending on the units being assessed.

Assessors must be trained and it is wise to have them meet the standards identified by the Training and Development Lead

Body. This move will give them and the candidates confidence in the system.

Assessors must have enough time, motivation and ability to take on the role, to interpret a new language and understand and maintain the recording system. Taking on such a role will also help their self-development and employment profile, aid them in the reappraisal and reorganisation of their own sections, and give formal recognition to a role which they may already be performing.

Perceived problems with the assessor system

The main worries we hear people expressing concern the costs, reliability and industrial relations implications of using line managers and supervisors as assessors. To take each of these in turn:

Costs

- Training costs will be high, especially in companies with high staff turnover, or little previous experience to build on.
- The costs of workplace assessments take the form of time – time away from the workplace, time spent on paperwork, time spent in extra meetings generated by deliberations, inter-assessor meetings to ensure consistency, meetings with the candidate.

Reliability

- Workplace assessors can be biased by their internal relationships with the staff.
- In some company cultures, work colleagues would not like to be put in the position of judging each other.

Industrial relations

- Should the new responsibilities of the assessors entitle them to more pay?
- If you decide to pay them more, how will you select your assessors?

- If assessors are paid according to productivity, how are they compensated for time away from their job role?
- Should you and can you lighten the workload of assessors to make up for their new responsibilities?
- Will sufficient numbers of the workforce want to become assessors?

Reducing costs and concerns

One false economy is to economise on the training of assessors. Training is essential to the success of the entire operation. Cut down on training and you will reduce confidence in the approach, cause frustrations and hostility brought on by misunderstandings and confusion, waste time and money through inefficient assessment, waste time and money explaining and re-explaining hazy concepts, and leave your assessors more open to accusations of subjectivity.

The correct approach is to invest in and update guidance materials and recording systems. Do not let participants store up information and expertise in their heads only, because each time you lose someone the learning process will have to be repeated.

Phase in the assessment system and the training of assessors so that every effort can be made to streamline it prior to its full-scale operation.

THE CORNERSTONES OF ASSESSMENT

The vital ingredient in the development of your assessment system has to be the quality of the standards themselves.

Performance criteria must be evaluative and critical to the performance of the element. Your assessment system will end up assuring competences your organisation does not require if the performance criteria are subject to constant misinterpretation (so many elements are to be found where the performance criteria describe a completely different function). The costs of running your system will mount up if you have specified too many performance criteria, written range statements that are exhaustive lists of every possible assessment situation (all of which will have to be catered for by a source of evidence whether actual or inferred), or include draft knowledge and understanding deriving from your standards-development which resembles a syllabus rather than the knowledge required for the element alone.

Being aware of the assessment implications of the way your standards are put together and resolving them are two different issues. An area of enormous difficulty for standards-developers is solving the problems that arise when agreement is being sought over range statements. This is where the workplace and its practices really do impinge upon the ideals and philosophies of the competence movement. Consultants are busy coming up with devices to settle conflicts over range, but in our experience solutions are more often than not the product of a healthy pragmatism.

Compiling your evidence specifications

The development of evidence specifications can only be undertaken in the context of a stable standards model and progression structure. By this we mean that:

- The standards have been finalised in light of your consultations and approved again by the working group responsible for them (to ensure that the changes have not arisen from any misinterpretation of the intentions of the standards and to allow their clarification).
- You have a clear implementation strategy which has been agreed by all major interest groups. A lead body will have to establish the structure of the qualifications framework which will be based on its standards. This will concentrate on the identification of the most likely areas of uptake, the levels of qualification needed, which units will be put together to create qualification and what these will be

called. In a company environment you will need to carry out a similar exercise. You must decide which grades of employees will be expected to attain which units and at what level, whether training should be provided for those who do not meet the standards at present and how to deal with the issue of pay for units achieved.

These decisions should be made before the development of assessment systems, otherwise your deliberations over how to assess people will be made in a vacuum and have no bearing on the realities of your work environment. Much time will be wasted in discussing evidence requirements if working groups are still unsure about how standards will operate in the company, which level each unit should be aiming for, who the units are directed at and in what combinations units will be available. The structure you determine will be modifiable until all the assessments have finally been piloted, but you must have a strategic framework to operate within. It will make decisions such as how to prioritise your standards-development work and testing requirements much easier to make.

Writing evidence requirements and guidance

The working group

Your working groups will provide the most suitable mechanism for producing evidence requirements. The group will now be familiar with the language, concepts and contents of standards, so the learning process will be shortened. To use them to best advantage:

- Select the four or five members who were most at ease with standards to form a core group.
- Supplement this group with three or four other people, perhaps future assessors or people who were particularly helpful during consultation. One or two people should be picked specifically to help with the knowledge evidence.

These new members should be:

- able to assimilate the new ideas and concepts quickly;
- less advanced in their career and, therefore, more conscious of the knowledge they need in order to be competent (more experienced practitioners often experience difficulties in explaining what makes them so capable when it has become almost instinctive).

Trainers should be brought in for the contribution they can make to decisions about assessment techniques rather than those concerning knowledge and understanding. Use other groups to verify the work of this new group as and when necessary.

Deriving the information

In earlier projects, it was common to derive the knowledge component of the standards separately from the evidence and assessment specifications. Knowledge was almost an afterthought to the main process. This probably reflected the confusions around the issue. Since then, some experts have been arguing that there should be no underpinning knowledge at all because it is inherent in the standards.

Knowledge is still derived in many projects by separate groups of individuals working in parallel with the main teams of standards-developers. This method of working runs contrary to the view that knowledge is an integral part of the contents of the performance criteria and is as essential a form of evidence of competence as performance evidence.

Our view is that knowledge is a vital ingredient of the evidence requirements of competence and should be derived as such through a consideration of its interdependence with the range statements and the evidence requirements. The working group should view one unit at a time and create all the evidence requirements simultaneously.

Many different techniques for deriving knowledge have been put forward in recent years but none stand out. They all revolve around the creation of matrices which mechanise the examination of the performance criteria against the range and decisions about differently defined classes of knowledge and how they can be used.

Effectively, there is no substitute for a concerted examination of the standards against your own requirements for assessment in the workplace and sufficiency of evidence. Typically, this will involve brainstorming, using possible assessment scenarios, and giving accounts of critical incidents and how they should be dealt with. Your decision about which techniques to use can only be made in the context of your organisation's individual requirements.

A brief warning about range statements

One of the major problems is overspecification. The sheer volume of possible range classes and of different instances included in them, means that it is more practical to suggest where the most critical class of assessment situations is likely to be. These are usually the most common situations encountered, or those deemed vital to differentiating between those who are competent and the rest. A critical class must be supported by performance evidence to prove competence.

Beware of ranges that look like a list of every possibility. Take a step back when you see one and ask what are the distinguishing groupings, processes, techniques or principles that might make the range more manageable and assessable in the context of your particular industry and company. This will be exactly the sort of decision you will be making when you create parallel units to reflect the industry with more accuracy than the template unit derived from functional analysis can.

THE WAY FORWARD

This stage in the standards-development path is the trickiest but also the most satisfying for all involved. At last your working groups can consider their own standards in light of the demands and diversity of the real workplace and get stuck into a more hands-on aspect of the work. Once you start to think about how standards will be assessed they become alive and exciting.

To keep the whole process under control:

- Accompany your work with frequent briefings and controlled publicity to people outside the process.
- Pilot your system for at least a year prior to the launch.
- Be methodical in your approach to identifying the evidence requirements to ensure their applicability, operational feasibility and cost-effectiveness.
- Don't be forced into launching before you are ready.
- Explore and find solutions to your industrial relations difficulties at the start of the project.

6

Winning the Argument: A Five-Point Plan for Convincing your Colleagues

Firms and organisations of all sizes and in all sectors will tell you that they want performance of work to higher standards from their people. But convincing senior management that the implementation of standards of competence is the best way of achieving this will be no easy matter. Not least because it will tend to be training professionals who first switch on to competence and these are not typically in a position to capture hearts and minds in the boardroom. The problem is that if those hearts and minds are not captured then the best that can be achieved are piecemeal gains in isolated areas, achieved at high costs to the managers defending them and the organisation paying for them.

On those occasions when the impetus comes from the top, it all too often takes the shape of a directive to achieve objective X by date Y. All of a sudden the achievement of the directive is paramount and its implications for the way in which the organisation is managed and led become only secondary considerations. Early converts to the philosophy and practices of occupational compe-

---

MAIN OBSTACLES TO THE INTRODUCTION OF OCCUPATIONAL STANDARDS

- Unwillingness to accept other people's ideas.
- Insufficient incentive to change.
- Inadequate development resource.
- No agreed human resources development policy.
- Lack of external advice and guidance.
- Lack of top management commitment.

---

tence have quickly learned to take an integrated and cautious approach to their introduction.

What does it take, then, to win the argument in favour of using standards to change the way assessment, reward, recruitment, progression and development are currently handled? There are five concepts that we consider essential in building a compelling case:

1 It is not a training initiative!
2 Focus on the benefits.
3 Beware of the outside world.
4 Stay strategic.
5 Don't run before you can walk.

These will now be considered in turn.

IT IS NOT A TRAINING INITIATIVE!

In most cases we know, the consideration of standards-setting as a training initiative has been the kiss of death or at least the cause of much delay and even more confusion than generally exists in this area. Standards are a change agent, a performance tool, a decision-making support system and many other things too. One thing they are not are training specifications. There are positive training and development spin-offs from their use – like clearer definitions of training need, a reliable and accurate framework of objectives for the trainer to work towards and design training inputs of one kind or another to meet – but generally these are not the cutting edge of the argument, so keep them secondary. These relationships are demonstrated in Figure 6.1.

FOCUS ON THE BENEFITS

Most change programmes fail because the people trying to make them work get bogged down in technical detail and don't spend enough time clarifying or promoting their benefits. All the evidence from early attempts to implement standards of competence suggests that the advantages of their use are quickly sidelined by more vigorous and obscure debates about the techniques for deriving them in the first place, eg who should be involved in the development process? what should be the trade-off between the way the organisation operates now and the way it would like to operate in the future? how broad should the key roles and units of competence be and what are the implications of this for assessment-systems design and costs? how many performance criteria should there be?

Of course, there has to be a place for this kind of discussion. Not all firms and organisations which use standards will choose to import the national standards set by the lead bodies. Many will want either to set their own or at least to pick and mix lead body standards with others they have developed themselves. However, if the attempt to introduce competence as a new way of organising and managing people is marked by overly vigorous arguments about functional analysis, performance criteria and range statements then it will quickly grind to a halt. Producing

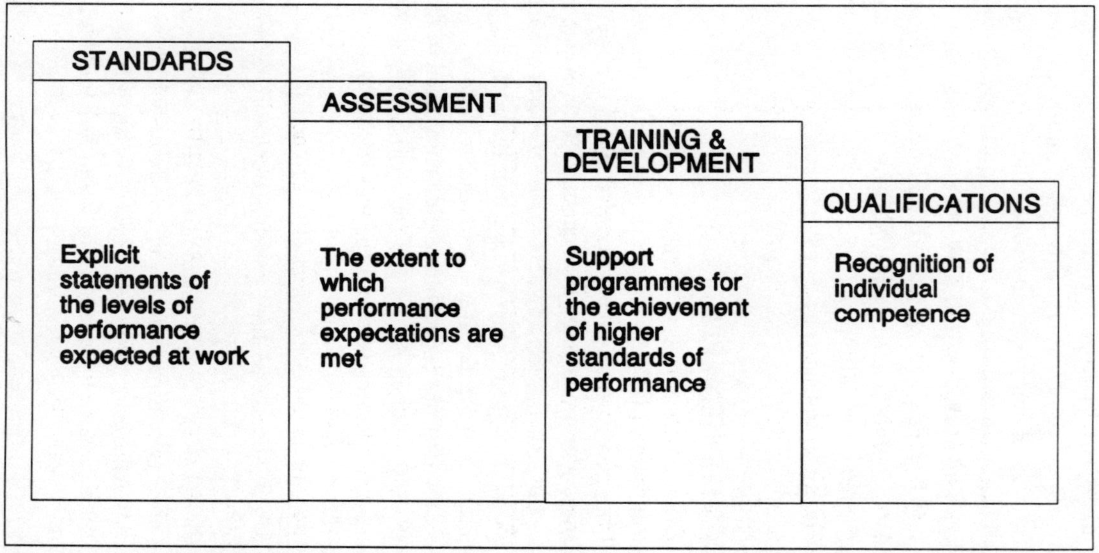

Figure 6.1 *Standards of competence in relation to assessment, training and qualifications*

STANDARDS	ASSESSMENT	TRAINING & DEVELOPMENT	QUALIFICATIONS
Explicit statements of the levels of performance expected at work	The extent to which performance expectations are met	Support programmes for the achievement of higher standards of performance	Recognition of individual competence

and communicating a strong needs-led rationale for reorganising the activities and management of the workforce using competence is much more important than winning a few methodological battles.

OPPORTUNITIES FOR ORGANISATIONS WHICH IMPLEMENT STANDARDS

- Focused training
- More consistent assessment
- Change-management tool
- Reward scheme framework
- Devolution of responsibility
- Initiative structuring
- Improved company performance
- Improved industrial relations

The two main reasons why organisations take standards of competence on board are motivation and the elimination of waste. As explained in Chapter 3, standards of competence are not a fancy new expression of the way things are done today, or have been done in the past. They are a strategic statement of what people should be able to do. As such they are orientated to the present and future workforce requirements of organisations. Furthermore, dynamic organisations regularly restructure and they alter their expectations of their people as they do so. Having a framework of standards in place against which all personnel are assessed provides a platform for the analysis, planning and control that the management of these kinds of organisation requires. It helps:

- to provide a more accurate picture of the deployment and total value of the human resource;

- to provide a sounder basis for managerial decisions about the future utilisation of human resources;
- to assist and evaluate the manpower benefits and costs of organisational planning and practices.

When organisations functionally analyse themselves and map the functions they need, they find that this map differs considerably from the type of organisational structures they currently operate and the jobs they support. All the more reason, then, to be clear about the benefits.

BEWARE OF THE OUTSIDE WORLD

Getting to grips with the many and varied strands of what is sometimes referred to as the 'competence movement' will be costly and frustrating. Moreover, you will probably feel very isolated – as if yours is the only organisation trying to make standards of competence happen in a real way. It is not simply a question of subscribing to the information databases of the NCVQ and SCOTVEC – they tell only part of the story. To appreciate fully the potential relevance of the standards and qualifications that either have been developed or are under development by the 160-odd lead bodies and industry training organisations will take time and patience.

Premature exposure of your organisation, particularly the people you are trying to switch on to competence, to the inconsistent quality and confusions of this outside world will almost certainly dampen their enthusiasm and raise their fears about costs and bureaucracy.

You will find that the majority of the obvious information sources available to you are geared to providing support and information linked to N/SVQs. The needs of the managers who are more concerned with getting standards of competence into their organisations, and who are not particularly fussy about those standards being the nationally agreed ones just so long as they meet the organisation's business needs, are only just starting to be realised. We have found that, without doubt, the best people for managers in this position to talk to are other managers who have gone through the same process. Typically, what they offer are approaches which put the benefits to the business of developing and using standards first, and the question of how the organisation might intercept a maturing NVQ framework a very definite second. There will be exceptions to this approach in certain sectors, particularly service ones where high volumes of new recruits are coming in with N/SVQs at level 2. But what most organisations are doing breaks down into three main stages:

- First, they are mapping the occupational functions they want (rather than those that they have at present).
- Second, they are matching their functional maps with the outputs of the lead bodies and ITOs.
- Third, they are taking their work forward by mixing imported standards – very typically in the areas of management and training – with others that they develop themselves.

By far the most important thing in all this is to get the competence philosophy accepted by a core team of influential managers who can then drive the development and implementation of standards for the workforce in general as part of an integrated, rather than isolated, strategy for improving efficiency, productivity and, of course, profitability.

STAY STRATEGIC

Standards of competence in all their various applications – assessment, job descriptions, N/SVQs, reward structures – are only the most visible part of the overall rethink that their successful introduction demands about the way organisations are managed, structured and led. It is not for nothing that some senior managers have dismissed them as subversive. Put quite simply, organisations that don't know where they are going or how they are going to get there are unlikely to derive much benefit from standards. This is because standards work best when linked to what an organisation wants to become rather than what it is today. Whatever happens, don't allow your organisation to drift into standards. Lots of organisations have done this in the past and paid the price and many more will do it in the future. Don't be one of them. Unless you adopt the same kind of strategic rigour in assessing the potential worth of taking standards on board, you will be fighting a losing battle from the day you start trying to find out what the fuss is all about until the day your senior management says enough is enough!

Standards are a useful contributor to planned organisational change. Wherever the consequences of a decision to change the way an organisation operates throws up questions about the way things are currently done and how jobs are performed there is a potential role for standards. Again, they are a useful way of focusing people's minds on the way things should be done rather than the way they always have been done.

Figure 6.2 illustrates the core processes of the competence-based approach. This is not a life-cycle model of standards-production and implementation. Instead, it places the emphasis on the interdependence of events which link and can provoke modifications to the performance of individuals in relation to the strategic needs and directions of organisations. By focusing on this rather than merely the technical components of the standards-development process, a clearer perspective can be gained on the capacity of competence to generate relevant specifications of learning needs, rational analysis of personnel deployment and clear expectations of job performance. The core processes of the competence-based approach fall into three main groups:

- Organisational context (needs generation).
- Standards development (needs definition).
- Individual development (needs communication).

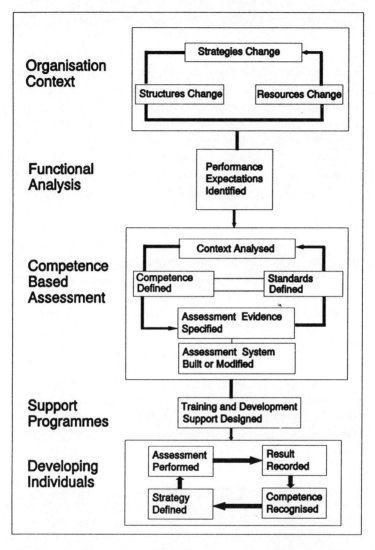

Figure 6.2 *Core processes of the competence approach*

Organisational context (needs generation)

This process generates the need for a competence-based approach. The key player is the organisation itself, which establishes the broad aims and constraints of the competence system regarding performance, progression, learning and assessment. The expression of these comes as a result of continuous and dynamic interaction between three sub-processes:

- **Changes in organisational strategy** may involve new business activities requiring employees to adapt to different work-roles.
- **Changes in organisational structure** may occur in response to strategic decisions or as a result of attempts to rationalise human resources and require employee adaptation to new situations, line management arrangements or work-roles.
- **Changes in the allocation of resources** could occur as a result of either of the above or a separate investment decision.

The outcome of any of these events will of course affect people's performance at work, their learning needs and the design of training programmes and also heavily influence the nature and scope of the standards-development and competence-based assessment system design activity.

Standards-development (needs definition)

This is the process which most directly affects the competence-based assessment system and corresponds most closely to the standards-development process described at length in other parts of this book. This is where the requirements stemming from the needs generation process are translated into the standards of competence which ultimately will enable learning, adaptation and better job performance to be achieved by the individual employee. It is better not to treat the sub-processes involved as discrete steps but see them as part of a lively dialogue. At the same time, they fall into two general areas which rotate around the stage in which assessment evidence is specified: prior to this stage, there is a series of highly interactive and iterative technical tasks; the work which comes after this follows a more linear, goal-orientated path.

Individual development (needs communication)

This is the point at which competence-based assessment goes live. Active line-manager communications and learning support are the crucial ingredients for making a success of it. Like needs generation, this is not a linear process but a cycle which continues until a particular aim is achieved and which can change direction or link into external processes like salary appraisal. It is possible for this cycle to be initiated by either the individual employee or the organisation, depending on which identifies the development need.

From the organisation's point of view, the aim of a competence-based assessment system is to fine-tune the performance at work of its employees to its needs. Positive change in the performance of just one employee improves the organisation's ability to respond to desired or dictated changes in strategy, structure or resources. The degree to which this happens is the main measure of the effectiveness of the competence approach.

DON'T RUN BEFORE YOU CAN WALK

The implementation of standards of competence is loaded with myriad implications for matters ranging from organisational structure, communications and management style, to production planning, human resource development and marketing. For this reason, it is crucial not to overestimate your capacity to bring about fundamental change in the way people work, are managed and are developed. Equally, it will be important to show how short-term as well as mid to long-term benefits can be gained by forays into standards-development. Focus on where the potential impact is greatest, where consensus is likely to be strong, workforce acceptance forthcoming, and the multiplier effects are most advantageous.

7

Implementing Standards of Competence: Putting Theory into Practice

THE HALLMARKS OF SUCCESSFUL IMPLEMENTATION STRATEGIES

We have taken a close look at the implementation experiences of organisations we have worked with over recent years and reached a number of conclusions about what distinguishes successful from unsuccessful attempts to implement standards. The history of unsuccessful attempts to introduce standards of competence on anything but a purely experimental scale suggests that they are characterised by:

- confused aims and objectives;
- more emphasis on structures and methods than on the benefits being sought and their link to the organisation's mission;
- resistance to change among managers, trainers and unions;
- a lack of knowledge and skills relating to the development and application of standards;

- under-budgeting of time and financial resources;
- selection of the wrong people to lead and participate in the initiative;
- not enough support from top management;
- the absence of quality documentation and information support; and
- poor housekeeping.

On the other hand, we believe that the more implementation conforms to the following guidelines, the greater its chance of success:

- beginning with a clear identification of the problems to be solved and an analysis of their broader context — taking into account technological, organisational, demographic, regulatory, human resource management and economic dimensions;
- identifying and meeting vital educational needs early in the process;
- cost-effectiveness;
- simple, well-designed and easily accessible information-support mechanisms and guidance materials which reflect the philosophy and strategy being followed and relate it to the core goals of the organisation;
- well-designed standards-development procedures, information systems and structures;
- strong co-ordination; and
- well-defined and communicated role and responsibilities allocation for all participants.

We have taken a close look at the implementation experiences of organisations we have worked with and talked to over recent years and believe that the more an implementation project conforms to the above guidelines, the more chance of success it is likely to have.

The rest of this chapter is devoted to the development of successful implementation strategies. Ultimately, of course, organisations will have to adopt unique approaches because their goals, strategies, structures, markets, resources and, above all, cultures will differ. As we have argued throughout this book, standards of competence are merely the tip of an iceberg atop a mass of human resource development, management and organisational issues. The greatest threat to their successful implementation in an organisation comes from people who insist from a purely technical point of view that they are the right solution. Although their intentions are good, their advice often leads to disappointment and disenchantment.

SIX STAGES IN THE IMPLEMENTATION OF STANDARDS

Standards of competence can be seen in a number of ways – as the basis of a system which enables organisations to take an entirely new approach to human resource development; as a supplement to already established approaches; or as an alternative to existing arrangements. How an organisation perceives their value and use depends on how it currently operates. Whereas some organisations will be attracted to a competence-based approach because it offers similar or better performance than current approaches, others will be judging the costs and resources required to implement one with no previous history of structured activities in this area.

We have divided the process of implementing standards of competence into six interlinking activities as follows:

- Scoping exercise.
- Detailed project planning.
- Developing standards and assessment systems.
- Consultation, testing and piloting.
- Introducing and maintaining standards.
- Evaluating the impact of standards.

Stage 1: Scoping exercise

This subject was briefly touched upon in Chapter 2. It is broadly the same as taking any other systems initiative from conception through to the design stage. In other words, you start by getting senior management on board. The purpose of scoping your organisation's potential commitment to a competence initiative is obvious. Projects or initiatives which aim to bring about quantitative and qualitative business improvements but start in the middle of nowhere, strategically speaking, will end up nowhere as well.

Adding to the complexity of considering the possible implications of going down the competence route are the inevitable internal and external interdependencies that will have to be taken into account when you first sit down to plan a way forward.

Start with a vision of the future

A vision of what your organisation wants to be in three to five years' time (or longer if you can manage it) is the best place to start the process of analysing, planning and communicating your needs and objectives. If one is not already in place then develop one. It doesn't have to be a one-sentence work of art – a general picture of what the organisation wants to achieve and how it wants its people to perform in the process will do. When you have something, pass it round your colleagues and senior management for comment. Until they believe in it, your initiative is not worth getting off the ground, and your case for change will lack bite.

This is also a good place to start because trainers, standards-developers and assessment-system designers use jargons that are alien to other parts of the workforce – particularly to line managers and their teams, where standards have most to contribute by way of improved communications and employee participation. Without a strong sense of the benefits to be gained by the introduction of standards and all the knock-on effects of this, mobilising support and commitment at any level will be very difficult and probably

short-lived. There is a long lead time before occupational standards and competence-based assessment systems reach the point
of introduction, and people have a tendency to forget why they
are doing things during it.

The virtues of a scoping exercise

Briefing senior management on the values and virtues of standards, training key personnel in standards-development techniques, and exposing the standards-developers themselves to the
details of the business are absolutely vital ingredients in this first
stage of the implementation process.

The core problem, however, is to determine the kind of standards an organisation needs and its people can use. It is not
enough merely to train a few well-placed managers and staff in
the art of standards-setting. While these people will quickly
become aware of the potential of competence, their detailed
appreciation of how to proceed will grow more slowly. They
need to be coached to the point where they can express the needs
of the organisation and their knowledge of its activities through
the functional analysis process, but in such a way that other managers and colleagues can still understand the performance specifications they either import from outside or design themselves.
The ways in which this process is planned, announced, docu-
mented, circulated and reported on must reflect this essential
relationship – between users who know the organisation and its
work, and standards-developers who know functional analysis
and what will and won't stand up in assessment. Systems analysts
have been trying to achieve a similar balance in the development
of computer systems for years. Going to senior management
without a clear idea of what it is you want them to support is
about as sensible as asking them to sign a blank cheque.

A short scoping exercise is a low-risk and effective way of
focusing your efforts in all these areas before your work starts in
earnest and the stakes rise. It should take 6 to 12 weeks to complete
and produce the following:

An identification of target workforce populations for the initiative
It might be everybody, it might be a more narrowly defined group. Either way, the reasons for selecting it should be spelled out in the context of your vision statement together with the implications of the choice.

An identification of main benefits being sought by the initiative
Try and break these down into primary and secondary, short and medium-term categories. Some examples of the kind of primary and secondary benefits identified by organisations we have dealt with in recent years are shown in the box below:

PRIMARY BENEFITS

- Raise commercial awareness of managers.
- Solve role ambiguities and so increase productivity.
- Empower people through self-development and the standards.
- Create a workforce which is demonstrably competent at all levels.
- A 'downsizing' tool which maintains gross productivity and improves quality.
- Use accreditation route to alleviating health and safety problems.
- Solid base for a credible continuing development policy.

SECONDARY BENEFITS

- Focuses training and development on specific occupational needs.
- Minimises use of external training resources.
- Provides good information base for manpower succession and continuity planning.
- Clarifies recruitment and selection processes.

The objectives of the initiative, an outline plan of action and a discussion of how you propose to approach it
Not just a rendition of your proposed methods and tactics for dealing with such things as meetings scheduling or authorisation of time away from the workplace, but a brief discussion of your strategy for achieving your objectives in such a way that the organisation gains the benefits it is seeking.

An estimate of the resources required by the initiative
Break these down into categories which make sense to your organisation, then run them month by month to produce a clear overview of the scale and intensity of the initiative.

An identification of the main interdependencies of the proposed initiative
It is difficult to exploit the advantages of standards of competence in stand-alone initiatives. Again, a few examples of the more common interdependencies identified by organisations we know of are shown in the box on the next page.

Identification of potential initiative champions and their props
Because of its potentially myriad interdependencies and organisational development implications, a standards initiative needs champions at every level, but especially at the top. The main roles of the champion are to:

- support and represent the initiative at all levels, but not lead it;
- raise profile of the standards initiative, both internally and in the outside world; and
- represent the organisation's point of view to the outside world (eg negotiations with professional, examining or awarding bodies).

In some organisations, particularly smaller ones, the choice of champion might appear to be made for you. Whatever the case, it is very important that you hold out for a champion whose previous championing has had good results, who is likely to see out the initiative, and who is embedded in the right internal and external networks.

INTERNAL INTERDEPENDENCIES

- Training and development programmes and policies.
- Common working practices.
- Management development framework incorporating an approach to the assessment of individual potential.
- Total Quality Management programmes.
- Downsizing plans and policies for the management of change.

EXTERNAL INTERDEPENDENCIES

- Investors In People awards.
- Training policies.
- Relevant lead body outputs.
- Previous standards-development experience.
- Professional body accreditation and registration policies.
- Overseas accreditation policies.
- Health and safety legislation.
- Equal opportunities.

The main danger in using champions is overloading them with information while trying to arm them with the appropriate arguments which help them avoid errors. For this reason, it is wise to provide a support person capable of translating the aims and objectives of the initiative into a language people at the highest level in your organisation can understand.

With this scoping exercise under your belt you should be in a strong position to articulate your proposition, support it by reference to the core business and its direction, and secure the resources you need to start the initiative proper.

A classic case of the benefit of hindsight - The lessons learned from an NVQ pilot project

Standards of competence raise issues that are at the very heart of organisations', development plans and policies. This is an area of extreme commercial sensitivity which means permissions for individual case studies are thin on the ground. Here, however, is a composite case we have put together out of the experiences and reflections of a number of organisations whose work in this area we know well.

The subject of our case is an organisation which provides services to large numbers of domestic customers in a region of the UK and employs around 3,000 people.

In 1990 it established a cross-functional working group to explore and develop the implications and consequences of implementing national standards and NVQs developed by lead bodies for all departments through a limited pilot exercise and recommend a corporate way forward. As the following extracts show, its final report identified three areas which had caused most problems, and which could have been avoided.

The role of managers

In the haste to start delivering NVQs corporately, the concerns that workplace supervisors and managers were to raise once the pilot had started were not adequately addressed. The working group thinks it should have met with the line managers and supervisors of the candidates, assessors and internal verifiers as soon as they had been identified. Then they could have been fully informed of the project's objectives and the vital support role that would be required of them. Instead, this task had to be tackled after the project commenced through a series of regular awareness sessions – a mechanism the working group considered only second best to meeting and winning the up-front commitment of the supervisors and managers of the employees actually using standards and pursuing NVQs in the pilot.

Timing

The rush to get the project underway also led to too much work having to be completed in too short a time. Two examples stood out:

(a) Enquiries from potential candidates for the pilot were numerous. It would have been more sensible to have held informal information sessions for potential candidates where enquiries, questions and concerns could have been aired. Everyone would have benefited from more explanation of the standards used. The related selection process for candidates requires a careful and planned approach, particularly in a corporate environment where equal opportunities considerations form an important element. Adequate time to discuss the project with more senior management representatives of departments also needs to be set aside at this stage

(b) As a result of the pressures resulting from the selection process, too little time was left to prepare for the formal training of assessors and internal verifiers.

Organisational implications

Any organisation embarking upon the use of national standards for workplace assessment needs to consider carefully the references which one finds in them to 'approved organisational manner, policy and procedures'. It is possible, particularly in an organisation with several hundred workplaces, that the perceptions of supervisors, managers, assessors and candidates about 'approved organisational manner' will vary significantly. One only has to consider the varying practices of organisations and individuals as they relate to answering the telephone to see the potential here for uncertainty in the application of consistent assessment procedures to all candidates. It is beneficial to study the standards closely before launching workplace assessment towards NVQs so that such matters can be properly addressed, rather than leaving some candidates unclear about the standards expected of them.

Stage 2: Developing a detailed project plan

The next phase of the initiative involves the production of a more detailed action plan. This is neither the time nor the place to elaborate on the fundamentals and techniques of project planning. Our assumption is that managers will already have these in place. On this basis, a detailed standards-implementation project plan should do at least the following things:

Develop an initial functional map of the organisation

The purposes and processes of functional mapping are discussed and described in considerable detail in Chapters 3 and 4. In summary, the production of an initial functional map is prerequisite to the planning of a standards-development and implementation programme. It expresses the occupational mix your organisation believes it needs to meet current and emergent organisational objectives.

A functional map will ultimately consist of a four-stage breakdown of the competences required into elements, but will usually stop short of defining performance criteria, although a lot of people are happy to proceed with a three-stage functional breakdown to unit level. The important thing is to see the functional mapping task as an early opportunity to get key people thoroughly acquainted with the functional analysis technique and the habit of thinking in terms of outputs and competences, rather than inputs, processes, job titles or existing organisational structures. It will also assist the planning and configuration of project working arrangements and resources as well as aid the identification and selection of externally produced standards of relevance to the organisation.

Identify your target populations

This is critical to the relevance and implementation prospects of standards-setting efforts in any organisation. When the time comes to introduce standards and competence-based assessment into the mainstream of an organisation's human resource development and management activities, a track record of goodwill and support from respected groups and individuals will be worth a thousand glossy presentations. It is vital to select a target population of potential participants in standards-development work, or candidates, assessors and verifiers for assessment pilots, who can make or are authorised to make time available to the project. But don't let the fact that some people have more time on their hands than others become the main selection criterion. The important questions and issues to consider are:

- The parts of the workforce most critical to your organisation's success now and in the future: What is the current and anticipated age/occupation mix and what will it be in five years' time? Where is the organisation most exposed to poor performance? Where is the organisation most likely to achieve a short-term return on its investment and demonstrate the future potential of standards-implementation?
- The strategic direction of the organisation: What is the core business? Is there a movement towards bigger or smaller units? Are there any plans to change the product – service mix?
- Where is the strongest, senior-level commitment to standards-development and implementation likely to come from? Remember you need champions at every level, especially at the top.
- What are the technical and organisational implications of different target groups?

- Don't stigmatise your initiative by concentrating on people involved in lower-level, largely routine jobs. It makes the people you choose feel that something is being done to them, and it makes the people you don't choose dismiss the initiative as irrelevant.

Detail a technical approach and communications programme

Again, Chapters 3 and 4 cover both of these issues in some detail. The important thing is to put some flesh on the bones of your approach by identifying by name the people you think should be involved and explaining why, and through a thorough analysis of the technical and communications options open to the organisation and their costs, produce a recommendation on the way forward. Pay particular attention to the education needs of the target audience for the project and of the wider workforce, not just to active members of your standards team. Initiative after initiative has suffered as a result of people being insufficiently informed about the motives of standards-development – which has a tendency to come across as a rationalisation tool, or an attempt to shift terms and conditions of employment in favour of the employer.

Resolve the key interdependencies

In stage 1 you will already have identified these. The task here is to identify the opportunities for integration so as to minimise waste in the system and maximise the benefits of proper co-ordination of complementary activities. As discussed earlier, the first place to look is among your organisation's training and development policies and programmes – especially those which centre on line management, communications and quality assurance.

Assessing individual performance against standards of competence gives organisations an opportunity to rethink their training and development activities completely. The onus is on the individual to demonstrate and evidence their competence to the assessor against clear criteria. The management role becomes that of creating an environment and decision-making framework

145

within which people can take responsibility and be accountable for their actions and where the emphasis is on progression through self-development. The focus is on learning rather than training programmes – an important shift in emphasis from the organisation to the individual which symbolises everything that standards of competence are about. In these circumstances, training design and delivery can be more flexible, more orientated to individual as well as group needs, and better integrated into the day-to-day responsibilities of line managers. The starting point for achieving these breakthroughs is assessor training to national standards for your line managers.

The seemingly obvious connections between competence and pay mean that you will have to think especially carefully about how you intend to proceed in this area and communicate your objectives to the workforce.

The larger your organisation, the more likely it is that someone somewhere has already been involved with a lead body or participated in a standards-development or testing exercise. Research this possibility carefully before going any further because, if they exist, these people's experiences, good or bad, planning.

Identify implementation scenarios and recommend budgets

This is a painful but essential part of the planning process. Your plan should provide top management with a detailed consideration of the downstream resource implications of pursuing standards-implementation. It is one thing to spell out the costs and time involved in getting standards and putting accompanying assessment systems into place. It is another to probe the resource requirements of operating, maintaining and updating these through to the medium term. To do this properly, you need to develop two or three implementation scenarios which put forward different ways in which standards might be introduced in your organisation, and to analyse their consequences.

Clearly, the consequences of a decision to introduce standards only partially will be different from those of a decision to go for a wholly integrated, top-to-bottom approach. Equally, the blend of internally set and nationally agreed standards you arrive at will influence how long and intensive the standards-development process is. The extent of your commitment to the emerging N/SVQ framework will also impact on the potential costs of assessment, record-keeping, certification and the external verification of your assessment systems. The permutations are endless. All that matters is that what you go with fits your organisation's particular interests, general attitudes and policies in these areas.

Identify important external information sources, networks and potential sources of expert support

As we write, the structure and availability of information and guidance on what is happening nationally are in a rather disorganised and confused state and generalisations about the range and quality of the service you could expect to encounter from lead bodies, ITOs, professional bodies, employer associations and so on are therefore risky. In these circumstances, the sensible things for you to do are to:

- clarify the information and guidance you will need on a regular and less regular basis. This will not only be in the form of printed matter, but could also be the names of people who are trying to do similar things to yourself;
- contact the lead bodies or ITOs or OSCs which seem most relevant to your organisation and request copies of the national standards they have published and the reports they have produced on such things as achieving consistent workplace assessment within their respective sectors. The vast majority of this is in the public domain and so should be made available to you at no or relatively little cost. Some of it is not and may be expensive. Some of it is being argued over and will be difficult to get hold of;
- contact your professional institution or institute and find

147

out what they are working on in this field and what support they can offer you. This is an obvious route for any organisation which has external accreditation arrangements for some of its training programmes with one or more of these bodies. Most of the professional bodies are now discussing the implications of the N/SVQ framework for their registration requirements and some, like the engineering ones, are actively involved in trying to make the relationships between the two more explicit;

- contact the N/SVQ officer at your local TEC or LEC and ask for details of its programmes and publications in this area. There might even be some money available to support your plans from this source, but beware – government money often comes with strings attached which may divert you from your true course!

- get in touch with local colleges and your chamber of commerce. A lot of colleges are licensed assessor centres for organisations like the MCI and so should be in a position to give you some information support;

- shortlist a few consultancies which might be able to assist at various points throughout the implementation process. Do not go straight for the cheapest. As always, the best way to choose consultants is by reference, reputation or personal experience. Remember, in the end you will work with an individual, or individuals, not their consultancy organisation. Don't just choose according to the consultancy's reputation – be aware of and specify the particular consultant you require. There are well over 400 consultants on the Department of Employment's database and the quality and breadth of their knowledge varies as greatly as their perspectives on standards;

- contact NCVQ or SCOTVEC, depending on your location, and ask for publication lists and subscription details for their qualifications databases;

- contact any awarding bodies with which your organisation already works closely and ask about current developments and what more they can do for you.

It's a familiar story: this is a growth area of activity but not all the key players in it are as proactive, customer centred or technically aware as they should be. So start your information-gathering and networking in places where you or your organisation already have good relationships, including inside the organisation itself. Pundits abound in this territory and if you are not careful you will lose sight of the wood for all the trees they insist on drawing your attention to.

Identify externally developed sets of standards of relevance to the target populations

This involves identifying potentially relevant lead bodies or ITOs and approaching them for copies of their published standards and qualifications frameworks, together with any guidance materials they may have. As indicated above, you might also find it useful to contact the Department of Employment, NCVQ, SCOTVEC and the National Council of Industry Training Organisations (see Appendix B for details) to gain some overview of what is happening nationally in the relevant areas.

The message contained in this book about the value to individual organisations in what is happening nationally is essentially a positive one. The extent to which an individual organisation wishes to comply with the rules and procedures pertaining to the award of N/SVQs based on the workplace assessment of people against national standards will determine the degree of effort it chooses to apply to identifying potentially relevant sets of national standards. Some employers have taken the view that it suits them better to develop their own standards and assessment systems – adopting and adapting units and elements of competence from national standards as appropriate – and link them to company-wide vocational qualifications. Others have done the same but leave it to individual employees to attain the unit accreditation they need for N/SVQs in their own time and at their own expense.

In the view of many employers, competence-based assessment is a more realistic and affordable proposition when freed from

N/SVQ quality assurance routines and all the costs and bureau-cracy associated with the awarding bodies' requirements to keep records in certain ways and engage in external verification of assessment systems. This may well change as the N/SVQ frame-work matures and external pressures on organisations to operate within it grow. In the meantime, the attitudes of employers like these are an important reminder to policy-makers in government and the key players that their role is to identify and respond to industry's needs.

When they first encounter national standards most managers complain of them being too open to interpretation. This is an inevitable result of efforts to ensure their transferability across firms and organisations of different kinds in a sector or across sectors which vary widely. There are procedures for customising national standards, but the degree of change that can be accom-modated within the criteria for N/SVQ assessment is really rather small. The amount of flexibility that organisations can expect on this matter is central to a lively debate which has been raging among key players on the national standards-development scene since the start. The accrediting bodies have been accused by many of dogmatically reinforcing the rules on assessment rather than focusing on the realities of what can and cannot be achieved in the workplace. This appears to be changing slowly and the rigid idea that entirely objective and consistent assess-ments can be carried out across whole organisations, let alone industries, is beginning to soften.

For the N/SVQ framework to function in the national interest it has to have rules and they should not change too often if employers, the employed and the unemployed are to gain confi-dence in this new currency for the labour market. Equally, the tremendous benefits associated with standards and competence-based assessment are only partially contained in the qualifica-tions. N/SVQs are only one component of self-development and a smaller part again of the organisational development gains to be made through the application of standards.

Stage 3: The development of standards and competence-based assessment systems

With a detailed plan and management support for it in place, the development process can now commence. This has been amply covered in earlier chapters and involves:

- Enacting the planned technical approach to deriving the standards by functional analysis.
- Meeting the identified education needs of target participants in the development process and the wider workforce – this will include organising assessor training for appropriate people.
- Implementing policy on the quality assurance of what is developed.
- Information-gathering and networking among key players on the national scene.
- Recording and collating the results of the standards-development process at every stage.
- Parallel development of assessment systems.
- Producing communications-support material, disseminating this and encouraging feedback on it through appropriate channels.
- Consulting and negotiating with trade unions as required.
- Notifying relevant professional institutions as appropriate.
- Monitoring and analysing implications for organisational development.

In parallel with the standards-development process, you might also initiate one or two investigations into such things as the efficiency and effectiveness of current assessment and appraisal systems, and the potential impact of standards on training and development policies, programmes and delivery.

Stage 4: Consultation, testing and piloting

Standards-development is a highly iterative and participative process. It is no different from any other new product or service development in the sense that the more potential users are involved in design and development, the more likely it is that the outcome will meet their needs and expectations.

The first time standards see the light of day is the point of no return for standards-developers. Up to this time, there are more variables under their control than otherwise. Beyond this point, it is the other way round and the reception given to the draft standards, prototype assessment systems and full-blown working models they produce is a clear barometer for the degree of success they can expect to enjoy.

If the education needs of relevant audiences have been properly attended to, if the initiative has been professionally and intelligently presented in the context of broader happenings within the organisation, if the difficult questions about pay and workforce numbers have been anticipated, and the technical quality of the work is right, then there is a more than fair chance of winning a lot of hearts and minds at this stage. Effectively, this what standards-testing is all about – exposing the logic and contents and ambition of the draft standards to a wider and less technically sympathetic audience.

Methods

Consultations occur whenever you need information from a wider audience. Generally, this will be during and after the standards development – as shown in Chapter 4 – and during and after the development of assessment systems. This section will briefly discuss the various tests you could use in these instances.

Once you have determined your technical approach and timescales, your next steps are to agree on a simple definition of what is proposed, which can be communicated across the workforce, and to make sure that project management procedures are clearly understood by all concerned. It is important that you understand the differences between consulting on the relevance and acceptability of the draft standards produced through stage 2, and field testing and piloting the standards – both of which occur later in the development path.

Consultations on draft standards

You should test the draft standards through consultation as soon as the development team is happy with them. The consultation process will test whether people are happy with their content and language. It will also serve to widen awareness and owner-ship of the standards.

Consultations typically involve combinations of the following techniques:

- Setting up new working groups to review the draft stand-ards critically.
- Running feedback workshops, organising discussion groups, making presentations to key groups, holding briefing sessions.
- Conducting formal surveys of opinion through question-naires and interviews.

The main task is to combine these in such a way that the consul-tation exercise does not just simply confirm the validity of the draft standards but actually challenges and refines them. Faced with a detailed and weighty set of draft standards, most people will be hard pressed to develop and justify arguments for change. One way of getting over this problem is to break the draft stand-ards up into smaller sets. Ensure that people understand they are faced with only one part of the standards and explain how they fit into the overall set. Another is to provide a helpline to guide them through any difficulties experienced in reading the stand-ards. You should not expect people outside the standards-development process to comment on the technical qualities of the standards. At this stage, these should be secondary to consid-erations of coverage, accuracy and presentation.

Who you choose to consult depends on which consultation techniques you employ, what you are asking for opinion on, and the degree of representativeness these factors enable and demand. For instance, managers are better at giving you feedback on the entire functional map, practitioners on the nitty gritty of the elements and performance criteria. Alternatively, if you are concerned that a working group has had a membership bias towards a specific occupational specialism, counteract this with a consultation group made of those who can balance the bias. A group meeting will be able to consolidate feedback for this balancing progress better than individuals replying to a questionnaire.

Field testing standards and assessment systems

Field testing will occur once the standards have been developed, and assessment systems and guidance on assessment have been put in place. The aim is to examine whether or not the standards, associated assessment methods, instruments and guidance are reliable, and the evidence they generate and assessors make judgements upon suits the organisation's purposes. It is also an opportunity to analyse the information-support requirements of the workforce. If your organisation is seeking to take N/SVQs fully on board, assessment systems and guidance have to comply with the quality-assurance procedures of the relevant awarding bodies.

Ideally, the people who take part in field tests should be new to the standards rather than converts, and the field tests themselves should occur under normal working and assessment circumstances. This will ensure that the standards can be used without special knowledge or detailed explanation. Field testing is another opportunity to impress new audiences with the relevance and utility of the standards and persuade them of the many benefits of applying them widely.

The typical components of a field test are:

- Defining samples and investigating access and availability issues with relevant managers.

- Selecting and training assessors, verifiers, workforce participants and mentors.
- Advance project-management briefing of participants.
- Testing the relevance of evidence specifications.
- Researching, developing and testing materials and procedures for meeting information and guidance needs.
- Establishing monitoring procedures and evaluation criteria.
- Modifying standards, assessment systems and guidance in the light of results.

Choose your sample carefully – its representativeness and depth in terms of the levels of the organisation it covers will be crucial to the case you construct in support of your organisation investing in the actual introduction and maintenance of a standards system – provided, of course, that this is the conclusion you reach.

It follows that the benefits and cost-effectiveness of introducing standards will have to be rigorously examined at the same time that the system's technical virtues are tested. The absolutely central questions to ask yourself here are: Exactly what contribution can standards make to the productivity and overall performance of the business? How much better are standards than alternative solutions to the same problem? Would the costs of introducing standards be outweighed by what they earned or saved over the medium term, and, if so, by how much and when?

Piloting

Once your competence-based system is developed, you need to consider how best to launch it. Piloting is a combination of final systems-testing and phased introduction. It should focus on the practicality of the standards in harness with your choice of assessment instruments and methods, verification, administrative arrangements and the integration of these into the mainstream policies and operations of your organisation. The results of a pilot should provide the final inputs to your business case for the adoption of a competence-based approach – with respect to its positioning within the organisation, its current and planned relationship to the N/SVQ framework, its cost and return goals, and the expected short and medium-term benefits. The typical components of a pilot are:

- Presentation of pilot aims, objectives and plan to all relevant parties.
- Selection and briefing of candidates and assessors.
- Assessor and verifier training.
- Pre-testing any externally marked written materials with candidates and assessors.
- Agreement of verification processes and procedures with management and with awarding bodies, if appropriate.
- Definition of evaluation criteria and monitoring arrangements.
- Modifications to standards and assessment systems in the light of evaluation.

If you are working towards the delivery of N/SVQs, then you should expect to work closely with one or more awarding bodies at this stage.

Your choice of pilot site will depend upon the strategic decisions you make concerning the scale and focus of the initiative as a whole, and will have resource and timescale implications for all of the above activities. There are three main options, and they are not mutually exclusive. Piloting could be taken forward:

- **On an individual site basis.** This option offers the potential benefits of being easier to organise, damage limiting and cheaper. Progress will probably be more rapid. The potential disadvantages associated with this option (dependent on core business/site correlation) are duplication in effort, less company-wide coherence and the danger of enshrining current site working practices.

- **On a company-wide basis.** If this option is adopted the advantages are minimisation of site-specific differences, maximisation of best practice, an increase in awareness and promotion of company-wide commitment. Unfortunately this strategy will be more expensive in both time and money, more difficult to organise both politically and logistically, and *not* market driven.

- **On a core business basis.** In most cases this is the option that we would advocate. It positions your initiative more explicitly as a change agent for the business and gives it a stronger market focus than technical focus, tying competence closer to broader efforts to achieve improved performance. This strategy would actively involve a body of personnel at all levels in the business in your initiative to improve the way they currently work and are organised. It would, however, also present major challenges to the business in terms of reorganisation, new thinking and overcoming resistance to change.

Industrial relations implications

Traditional, academic and time-based qualifications have always differentiated between those involved in skilled and managerial functions from those tending towards routine, unskilled ones. At the same time, they have also served to reinforce social status. So it is only to be expected that changing the terms of accreditation in the working environment (whether the accreditation be nationally recognised or company-wide) will have repercussions far beyond that environment and influence the degree of acceptance or rejection of the standards movement.

Regardless of how much common ground might exist in any particular situation, employers and employees have essentially different interests. A key element in the traditional employment contract is the emphasis placed by employers on minimum conditions of employment performance, which only loosely point to intended roles and responsibilities rather than precisely defining them. In this way, the employer can maintain considerable flexibility in applying the employee's labour. The employee, on the other hand, has a vested interest in formality at the level of the employment contract, and in accreditation and assessment which is linked to general rather than specific performance indicators. It follows that establishing standards of competence as the basic currency of performance assessment and progression – rather than sticking to traditional benchmarks such as apprenticeships, management diplomas, degrees or professional qualifications – will rely heavily on the extent to which the self-interests of employers, employees, educators and trainers alike can be harnessed.

Stage 5: Introducing and maintaining standards of competence

Parts of your organisation will almost certainly consider your plans for the introduction of standards as intrusive and threatening to the established order of things. You can expect vested interests to be stoutly defended even at this late stage. The extent to which this is still a problem will depend on how well the standards-development process was explained and marketed internally.

Standards-developers at national and organisational levels typically conceive of their efforts as innovative and helpful and find it hard to understand why others reject something so obviously value-adding. This is because they very often neglect the political dimension in their work – winning hearts and minds, persuading and convincing colleagues, constructing and demonstrating a powerful business case for the investments involved. They also underestimate the social and cultural changes that the embracing of competence philosophy entails. Standards can come across as an attack on the trust and confidence that has grown up between managers and subordinates and between colleagues over years. The way people work has as much to do with what they are prepared to do and the way they want to do things as with the way they are instructed or encouraged to do them. Even if standards are not intended to do these things, they will be regarded by some as if they were.

The key issues to be sensitive to when considering the launch of a competence-based system are how and at what rate the organisation can accommodate it, and how it can best be promoted. The previous stages of your work should have gained competence an important foothold in the organisation by establishing its feasibility, testing its practicality and demonstrating its benefits. However, most improvement programmes fail despite having achieved this. Introducing and maintaining a standards-based approach to generating higher levels of self-motivation, flexibility and performance in the workforce requires a mix of top-down and bottom-up tactics. The things to bear in mind as you wrestle with the questions of how to sustain the initiative and how long it will take for a competence approach to take hold are:

- The more senior the level of support for the introduction of competence, and the more serious management are about making it work, the more likely it is to gain initial acceptance.
- The more understanding the workforce has of the implications, the higher its commitment and acceptance levels will be.
- The more the advantages of introducing competence are seen to outweigh the costs, the more widespread commitment to it will be.
- The people you choose as champions, working group leaders and members; the ways in which you go about your consultation, field testing and piloting exercises; the content and professionalism of your presentations to senior management and other sections of the workforce; and the connotations you give to competence are all determinants of how much credibility the systems you have developed will have. The less its credibility, the shorter-lived and less beneficial the system will be.
- The more stringent and performance driven your monitoring and evaluation of a competence-based system, the greater the chances that it can play a strategic role within

the organisation and the longer it is likely to last.

- The greater the number of people involved as candidates, assessors, mentors, verifiers, reviewers and project workers within the system, the easier it will be to sustain.

- The more flexibility and responsiveness to administrative and assessment problems the system displays, the more relevance it will have. Central to this flexibility are clear policies and mechanisms for updating and reviewing the relevance of the standards themselves, which should extend to regular consideration of the relationship your system has with awarding bodies and the N/SVQ framework.

- The better the communications, support materials and mechanisms, co-ordination and information flows of the system, the more support it will get.

Stage 6: Evaluating the impact of standards

The role and context of evaluation

Evaluation is a vital part of the process of developing and implementing standards of competence. Properly carried out, it can ease the introduction of standards, help to define the nature and scope of the task and ensure that lessons learned along the way are retained for later use. In short, evaluation helps you to get where you are going, and understand if it is as good a place as you expected.

Whenever managers consider introducing new forms of organisation or restructuring, the central concerns are efficiency and rationality. Efficiency is the ability to generate levels of productivity in keeping with the opportunities and constraints of the market. Rationality is the extent to which any organisation structures itself internally in response to those same external opportunities and constraints. In recent years, and especially in today's economic climate, more and more large private and public sector organisations have been decentralising or undertaking other forms of restructuring to reduce the increasing costs of central co-ordination and functional specification, while smaller ones have been eschewing traditional hierarchical arrangements for more innovative structures to keep overheads to a minimum and optimise customer sensitivity.

Whatever their motivation, changes in operating structure such as those which can result from standards-implementation may prove costly in the short run but efficient in the medium to long term. The evaluations you conduct in the consultation, field testing and piloting stages should reflect the complex internal and external consequences of change on this scale, and the inevitability that your case for the introduction of a competence-based approach will be appraised in this light. So should your ongoing evaluation of the impact of standards as they are being introduced to the workplace. It is particularly important to keep re-evaluating your budget projections, and carefully examining the impact of competence on other important internal initiatives and external arrangements (accreditation, recruitment, reward schemes etc).

Evaluation planning

There are three main things to remember when planning to evaluate the impact of standards, whether they are under development or about to be implemented in the workplace:

1 Identify and involve key interest groups – those whose interests are directly affected in one way or another by the introduction of standards of competence. This will give credibility to your evaluation work, assist the flow of feedback and information it needs and make its results more relevant.

2 Different interest groups are convinced by different types of approaches and results – for example, if you are evaluating the progress or results of an assessment system pilot exercise, you might need to produce technical evidence for

personnel specialists and a cost–benefit analysis for your managers.

3 The process of implementing standards of competence is an innovative one. The plans you make and the goals you set at the outset will change over the course of your work. Carefully targeted evaluation can help you respond to and understand the implications of this.

Approaches to evaluation

To deal adequately with the complexities of this task, you should combine formative and summative approaches.

Formative evaluation

The main aim of this approach is the proper structuring of your objectives at every stage of your work from initial standards-development, through testing to actual standards-implementation in the workplace, and to measure progress against them on an ongoing basis.

To achieve this, an evaluation framework should first be established. This normally involves synthesising your objectives into a project-management grid. This will provide a detailed breakdown of your objectives and a list of the key questions about the value standards are actually adding to your business along the way.

The benefits of the formative approach are threefold:

1 It combines a qualitatively driven framework with quantitative measures for maximum impact on the way projects are managed and implemented.
2 The project management team will be able to use the framework to synthesise more easily the data and information that is fed back to them. This will also assist the team to identify gaps in the evaluation process.
3 It will help all projects in the early detection of problems, in the internal communication of objectives and in management decision-making.

A version of the common evaluation framework should be produced early in the life of your project. This can then be modified with input and critique from your project teams through discussion. From this point on, the framework should be modified regularly as the project progresses.

The final version of the framework can then serve as a reference tool for your summative evaluation as well as a guideline for future projects.

Summative evaluation

The main aim of this approach is to report on outcomes and impact at the end of each stage of your work. A summative evaluation should cover:

- needs analysis;
- objectives definition;
- action planning;
- implementation of actions;
- success of actions; and
- future decision-making.

It should take as its starting point the final version of the formative evaluation framework. A list of key questions should then be developed which are likely to include:

- Have the needs which the standards-initiative is responding to been given the same level of priority by all levels of management?
- How do project objectives, actions and results compare across the organisation?
- At a project level, how do planned and actual actions compare?
- What factors most influenced the process of translating plans into actions and the results of these?

8

Future Directions

It has been said that the introduction of standards of competence into any organisation, large or small, is as complex and unpredictable as letting a drop of red dye drip into a glass of water.

The decision to use standards will certainly affect businesses in areas of great complexity and sensitivity – communications among colleagues, relationships between management and the workforce, the way work is organised, and the confidence the organisation has in its ability to achieve its objectives.

Introducing change always has had its risks and uncertainties. As every manager knows, you can only predict so many of the outcomes of any new venture, be it a new product or a reorganisation. You can only predict so many of the benefits as well. And sometimes, you can only find out if something works by trying it.

Not that the introduction of standards should be quite the leap in the dark that the opening remark of this chapter suggests. Standards are a very powerful organisational development tool indeed and should be treated with respect from the start. So don't pigeon-hole them as a training tool, don't waste their potential by confining their application to your youth training involvements or never-ending experiments on the shopfloor or in the office, and don't let your managers escape the focus and disciplines that standards can bring to the way they are organised and do their jobs.

Developing your own standards of competence can be an extremely rewarding process, forcing taboos to be broken, long-standing problems to be resolved, all forms of comfort blanket to be burned, and the unthinkable to be thought. Manage this process carefully. Here are some dos and don'ts to bear in mind:

- Don't keep the development work to yourself and a favoured few or there is a strong possibility that your standards will be disowned.
- Don't involve too many people or there is the equally strong likelihood that your development work will be crushed under a weight of logistics, functional analysis training and political in-fighting.
- Do make judicious use of the standards, assessment and implementation guidance being produced by the lead bodies, ITOs, the NCVQ, SCOTVEC and all the other external parties mentioned earlier in this book. Despite the apparent confusions in the way their work is being organised at the national level, and the teething troubles that are inevitable for any initiative of this size, there is some excellent material to be drawn upon, regardless of whether it entirely or only partially meets your needs.
- Do be aware of what you want, why you want it and where it is taking you. This is crucial; if your organisation is unclear on any of these counts, then it should keep its distance from competence.
- Do put good people on the job – give the task of translating what is happening nationally, in the sector or in the occupational areas which affect your organisation most, to people who have a good understanding of the way the organisation works, what its vision is, how it intends to get there, and the way its markets operate. Standards-development needs to be in the hands of motivated people who care about these things, can quickly see where standards can make a contribution and have the presence to sell

this message to their bosses, their colleagues and their subordinates.

We are on the verge of an explosion in the take-up of standards of competence, both the nationally agreed ones developed by lead bodies and the company-specific ones developed by organisations which prefer to go that way. Such is the level of interest and business commitment to the use of occupational standards at this relatively early stage in their emergence. This explosion will be initiated not by the emergent N/SVQ framework but by the benefits and utility inherent in the competence-based approach. Managers at all levels will be able to use standards to assess and influence the performance and development needs of their people. This will reduce the traditional dependence that managers in larger businesses have on their training and personnel departments, and add a new dimension to the activities of most smaller firms. Meanwhile, the use of common standards and assessment methods will ensure that overall coherence and control can be maintained. Instead of relying on technical specialists to implement systems for measuring and monitoring the effectiveness and deployment of the workforce in relation to its objectives, a business will be able to rely on its own managers to do this in line with its strategic planning.

Standards of competence will close the gap between strategic planning and implementation that most businesses suffer from. This will cut down delays in communicating strategic change to the workforce, quicken the response rate to external forces, ensure that everyone in the organisation is clear about its objectives and the implications these have for their self-development, and enrich the impact of systems and product-quality standards by explicitly targeting the performance of people.

Central to this breakthrough are important changes in the way line managers are seen by senior management, the people who report to them, and by themselves. No longer will job descriptions, centralised training and development arrangements, or traditional assessment and appraisal systems get in the way of organisational change. In the course of setting or selecting standards of competence for their own use, businesses will come to see themselves in a new light, where occupational functions, organisational structures and job-performance expectations will be linked to what needs to be done from a strategic, market-related perspective rather than a historical one. Once standards of competence are in place, their relevance to this changing strategic, market perspective will need to be continually reviewed. This will provide all levels of management with regular opportunities to examine the adequacy of existing organisational arrangements and performance expectations. Previously developed standards will then be used as a basis for updated ones which target the new circumstances.

We hope that this book encourages you to explore standards of competence for the first time, take fresh heart if you have had early setbacks, or work more confidently to persuade colleagues and senior management that there are benefits to your organisation in this area and that it's time to start trying to reap these before your competitors do.

APPENDIX A

Lead Bodies and Industry Training Organisations

There follows a list of names and addresses of organisations which act in the capacity of lead bodies and industry training organisations. There are two types of lead body: sectoral ones and cross-sectoral ones. Both develop national standards and design N/SVQs based on these. Industry training organisations have a wider remit, including promoting and marketing the standards and qualifications and analysing skill shortages within their sectors.

Most of these organisations should be able to field your enquiries, and the majority should be in a position to supply you with copies of standards, assessment guidance, implementation plans, case studies or other reports for the occupational areas they operate in. We have checked the details in the following list very thoroughly but cannot guarantee that they will be correct at the time of publication.

AEA Technology (Atomic Energy), Corporate HQ, Harwell, Didcot, Oxfordshire, OX11 0RA. Tel 0235 433689.

Agricultural Co-operatives Training Council, 23 Hanborough Business Park, Long Hanborough, Oxford, OX8 8LH. Tel 0993 883577.

Agricultural Training Board, Head Office, Stoneleigh Park

Pavilion, Kenilworth, Warwickshire, CV8 2UG. Tel 0203 696996.

Animal Care Lead Body, Wood Green Animal Centre, Kings Bush Farm, London Road, Huntingdon, Cambridgeshire, PE18 8LJ. Tel 0480 831177.

Arts & Entertainment Technical Training Initiative, Silverton Cottage, High Street, Broughton, Hants, SO20 8AD. Tel 0794 301386.

Arts and Entertainment Training Council, 3 St Peters Building, York Street, Leeds, LS9 8AJ. Tel 0532 448845.

Association of Accounting Technicians, 154 Clerkenwell Road, London, EC1R 5AD. Tel 071 837 8600.

Association of British Travel Agents National Training Board, Waterloo House, 11–17 Chertsey Road, Woking, Surrey, GU21 5AL. Tel 0483 727321.

Association of the British Pharmaceutical Industry, 12 Whitehall, London, SW1A 2AY. Tel 071 930 3477.

Autoclaved Aerated Concrete Products Association, c/o Tarmac Topblock Ltd, Roadstone House, PO Box 44, 50 Waterloo Road, Wolverhampton, West Midlands, WV8 2HZ. Tel 0902 754131.

Aviation Training Association, 125 London Road, High Wycombe, Buckinghamshire, HP11 1BT. Tel 0494 445262.

Banking Lead Body, Banking Information Service, 10 Lombard Street, London, EC3V 9AT. Tel 071 626 9386.

Basket Makers' Association, Millfield Cottage, Little Hadham, Ware, Hertfordshire, SG11 3ED. Tel 0279 51497.

Biscuit, Cake, Chocolate & Confectionery Alliance, 11 Green Street, London, W1Y 3RF. Tel 071 629 8971.

Book House Training Centre, 45 East Hill, Wandsworth, London, SW18 2QZ. Tel 081 874 2718.

Booksellers Association, Minster House, 272–274 Vauxhall Bridge Road, London, SW1V 1BA. Tel 071 834 5477.

Brewers Society, 42 Portman Square, London, W1H 0BB. Tel 071 486 4831.

British Agriculture and Garden Machinery Association, 14 Church Street, Rickmansworth, Hertfordshire, WD3 1RQ.

Tel 0923 720241.

British Box and Packaging Association, Papermakers House, Rivenhall Road, Westlea, Swindon, Wiltshire, SN5 7BA. Tel 0793 886086.

British Brush Manufacturers Association, Book House, 4 The Lake, Bedford Road, Northampton, NN4 0YD. Tel 0604 22023.

British Cement Association, Century House, Telford Avenue, Crowthorne, Berkshire. Tel 0344 762676.

British Coal, Eastwood Hall, Mansfield Road, Eastwood, Nottingham, NG16 3EB. Tel 0773 532111.

British Fibreboard and Packaging Association, 2 Saxon Court, Freeschool Street, Northampton, NN1 1ST. Tel 0604 21002.

British Footwear Manufacturers' Federation, Royalty House, 72 Dean Street, London, W1V 5HB. Tel 071 734 0951.

British Furniture Manufacturers' Federation, 30 Harcourt Street, London, W1H 2AA. Tel 071 724 0854.

British Gas, 3rd Floor, 100 Rochester Row, London, SW1P 1JB. Tel 071 821 1444.

British Institute of Professional Photography, Fox Talbot House, 2 Amwell End, Ware, Hertfordshire, SG12 9HN. Tel 0920 464011.

British Jewellers Association, National Joint Working Group for the Jewellery & Allied Industries, 10 Vyse Street, Birmingham, B18 6LT. Tel 021 236 3393/2657.

British Landscaping ITO, Landscape House, Henry Street, Keighley, West Yorkshire, BD21 3DR. Tel 0535 606139.

British Leather Confederation, Leather Trade House, Kings Park Road, Moulton Park, Northampton, NN3 1JD. Tel 0604 494131.

British Marine Industries Federation, Meadlake Place, Thope Lea Road, Egham, Surrey, TW20 8HE. Tel 0784 473377.

British Narrow Fabrics Association, c/o KLITRA, 7 Gregory Boulevard, Nottingham, NG7 6LD. Tel 0602 623311.

British Nuclear Fuels, Risley, Warrington, Cheshire, WA3 6AS. Tel 0925 832000.

British Paper and Board Industry Federation, Papermakers House, Rivenhall Road, Westlea, Swindon, Wiltshire, SN5 7BE. Tel 0793 886086.

British Pest Control Association, 3 St James Court, Friargate, Derby, DE1 1ZU. Tel 0332 294288.

British Plumbing Employers Council (BPEC), c/o SNIPEF, 2 Walker Street, Edinburgh, EH3 7LB. Tel 031 225 2255.

British Polymer Training Association, Coppice House, Halesfield, Telford, Shropshire, TF7 4NA. Tel 0952 587020.

British Ports Industry Training Ltd, PO Box 555, Bury St Edmunds, Suffolk, IP28 6QG. Tel 0284 811555.

British Printing Industries Federation, 11 Bedford Row, London, WC1R 4DX. Tel 071 242 6904.

British Rail, Euston House, 24 Eversholt Street, PO Box 100, London, NW1 1DZ. Tel 071 922 4125.

British Sign Association, Swan House, 207 Balham High Road, London, SW17 7BQ. Tel 081 675 7241.

British Soft Drinks Association, 20–22 Stukeley Street, London, WC2B 5LR. Tel 071 430 0356.

British Steel Plc, Ashorne Hill Management College, Leamington Spa, Warwickshire, CV33 9QW. Tel 0926 651321.

British Timber Merchants' Association, Stocking Lane, Hughenden Valley, High Wycombe, Buckinghamshire, HP14 4JZ. Tel 0494 563602.

British Waterways Board, Willow Grange, Church Road, Watford, Hertfordshire, WD1 3QA. Tel 0923 226422.

Broadcasting, Film and Video Industry Training Organisation (SkillSet), Channel 4 TV, 60 Charlotte Street, London, W1P 2AA. Tel 071 927 8568.

Building Products Training Council, c/o CITB London & South East Region, Radner House, 1272 London Road, Norbury, London, SW16 4EL. Tel 081 679 8511.

Building Societies Association, 3 Savile Row, London, W1X 1AF. Tel 071 437 0655.

Bus and Coach Training Ltd, Gable House, 40 High Street, Rickmansworth, Hertfordshire, WD3 1ER. Tel 0923 896607.

Caravan Industry Training Organisation, Catherine House, 74–76 Victoria Road, Aldershot, Hants, GU11 1SS. Tel 0252 344170/318251.

Care Sector, Consortium (NHSTD), St Bartholomews Court, 18 Christmas Street, Bristol, BS1 5BT. Tel 0272 291029.

Carpet Industry Training Council, 39 Knox Chase, Harrogate, North Yorkshire, HG1 3HL. Tel 0423 502413.

Carpet Industry Training Council, c/o British Carpet Manufacturers Association, 4th Floor, Royalty House, 72 Dean Street, London, W1V 5HB. Tel 071 734 9853

CATITO, (Cotton and Allied Textiles Industry Training Organisation), Reedham House, 31 King Street West, Manchester, M3 2PF. Tel 061 832 9291.

Association for Ceramic Training & Development, 2nd Floor, Federation House, Station Road, Stoke on Trent, Staffordshire, ST4 2SA. Tel 0782 745335.

Chemical Industries Association, Kings Buildings, Smith Square, London, SW1P 3JJ. Tel 071 834 3399.

China Clay and Ball Clay Industries Training Board, John Keay House, St Austell, Cornwall, PL25 4DJ. Tel 0726 74482.

Cleaning and Support Services Association, Suite 73/4, The Hop Exchange, 24 Southwark Street, London SE1 1TY. Tel 071 403 2747.

Cleaning Industry Lead Body, Hill House, Skinners Lane, Wroxham, Norwich, Norfolk, N12 8SJ. Tel 0603 784547.

Clothing and Allied Products Industry Training Board (CAPITB Trust), 80 Richardshaw Lane, Pudsey, Leeds, LS28 6BN. Tel 0532 393355.

Concrete Industry Lead Body Secretariat, Pre-Cast Concrete Industry Training Association, 60 Charles Street, Leicester, LE1 1FB. Tel 0533 512442.

Confederation of British Wool Textiles, Merrydale House, Roydsdale Way, Bradford, West Yorkshire, BD4 6SB. Tel 0274 652207.

Construction Industry Standing Conference, The Building Centre, 26 Store Street, London, WC1E 7BT. Tel 071 323 5270.

Construction Industry Training Board, Bircham Newton, Kings Lynn, Norfolk, PE31 6RH. Tel 0553 776677.

Convention of Scottish Local Authorities, Rosebery House, 9 Haymarket Terrace, Edinburgh, EH12 5XZ. Tel 031 346 1222.

Cosmetics, Toiletry and Perfumery Association, 35 Dover Street, London, W1X 3RA. Tel 071 491 8891.

COSQUEC, (Council for Occupational Standards and Qualifications in Environmental Conservation), The Red House, Pillows Green, Staunton, Gloucestershire, GL19 3NU. Tel 0452 840825.

Cotton & Allied Textiles Industry Training Organisations, Reedham House, 31 King Street West, Manchester, M3 2PF. Tel 061 832 9291.

Dairy Trade Federation, 19 Cornwall Terrace, London, NW1 4QP. Tel 071 486 7244.

Direct Selling Association, The Sales Lead Body, 29 Floral Street, London, WC2E 9DP. Tel 071 497 1234.

Distilling Industry, Vocational Qualifications Group, 20 Atholl Crescent, Edinburgh, EH3 8HF. Tel 031 229 4383.

Electrical and Electronics Servicing Lead Body, c/o EEB, Savoy Hill House, Savoy Hill, London, WC2R 0BS. Tel 071 836 3357.

Electrical Installation Engineering Industry Training Organisation, ESCA House, 34 Palace Court, London, W2 4HY. Tel 071 229 1266.

Electricity Training Association, Industrial Relations Department, 30 Millbank, London, SW1P 4RD. Tel 071 834 2333.

Emergency Fire Industry Services Lead Body, Home Office Room 935, 50 Queen Anne's Gate, London, SW1H 9AT. Tel 071 273 3925.

Engineering Construction Industry Training Board, Blue Court, Church Lane, Kings Langley, Hertfordshire, WD4 8JP. Tel 0923 260000.

Engineering Occupations Standards Group, The Engineering Council, 10 Maltravers Street, London, WC2R 3ER. Tel 071 240 7891.

Engineering Services Standing Conference, The Institute of Marine Engineers, The Memorial Building, 76 Mark Lane, London, EC3R 7JN. Tel 071 481 8493.

Engineering Services Training Trust Ltd, ESCA House, 34 Palace Court, Bayswater, London, W2 4JG. Tel 071 229 2488.

EnTra (Engineering Training Authority), Vector House, 41 Clarendon Road, Watford, Hertfordshire, WD1 1HS. Tel 0923 238441.

Fabric Care Research Association Ltd, Forest House Laboratories, Knaresborough Road, Harrogate, North Yorkshire, HG2 7LZ. Tel 0423 885977.

Federation of Bakers, 20 Bedford Square, London, WC1B 3HF. Tel 071 637 7575.

Fibre Cement Manufacturers Association, PO Box 117, Hexham, Northumberland, NE4 63Q. Tel 0434 601393.

Fire Industry Lead Body, The Loss Prevention Council, 140 Aldersgate Street, London, EC1A 4HX. Tel 071 606 3757.

Floristry Industry Vocational Qualifications Group, College of NE London, Tottenham Centre, High Road, Tottenham, London, N15 4RU. Tel 081 802 3111.

Food and Drink Consortium, 6 Catherine Street, London, WC2B 5JJ. Tel 071 836 2460.

Food Manufacturers' Council for Industrial Training, 6 Catherine Street, London, WC2B 5JJ. Tel 071 836 2460.

Footwear Repairs, 76 The Parade, Sutton Coldfield, West Midlands, B72 1PD. Tel 021 355 2033.

Foreign Airlines Training Council, c/o Air France, Colet Court, 100 Hammersmith Road, London, W6 7JP. Tel 081 742 6600.

Forensic Science Service, Priory House, Gooch Street North, Birmingham, B5 6QQ. Tel 021 666 6606.

Forestry & Arboriculture Safety Training Council, Forestry Commission, Room 413, 231 Corstorphine Road, Edinburgh, EH12 7AT. Tel 031 334 8083.

Forestry Training Council, Room 413, 231 Corstorphine Road, Edinburgh, EH12 7AT. Tel 031 334 0303.

Gamekeeping and Fish Husbandry, Meadow Down,

Basingstoke Road, Old Alresford, Hampshire, SO24 9DS. Tel 0962 734019.

Glass Training Ltd, BGMC Building, Northumberland Road, Sheffield, S10 2UA. Tel 0742 661494.

Hairdressing Training Board, 3 Chequer Road, Doncaster, South Yorkshire, DN1 2AA. Tel 0302 342837.

Health and Beauty Therapy, (HBTTB) PO Box 21, Bognor Regis, West Sussex, PO22 7PS. Tel 0243 860339.

Heating and Ventilating Contractors Association, ESCA House, 34 Palace Court, London, W2 4JG. Tel 071 229 2488.

Hire Association Europe Ltd, 722 College Road, Erdington, Birmingham, B44 0AJ. Tel 021 377 7707.

Hotel and Catering Training Company, International House, High Street, Ealing, London, W5 5DB. Tel 081 579 2400.

Incorporated National Association of British & Irish Millers, 21 Arlington Street, London, SW1A 1RN. Tel 071 493 2521.

Industry Lead Body for Design, 29 Bedford Square, London, WC1B 3EG. Tel 071 631 1510.

Information Technology Industry Training Organisation, ITILB Secretariat, 16 South Molton Street, London, W1Y 1DE. Tel 071 355 4924.

Institute of Chartered Secretaries and Administrators, Administration Lead Body, 16 Park Crescent, London, W1N 4AH. Tel 071 580 4741.

Institute of Maintenance & Building Management, Keets House, 30 East Street, Farnham, Surrey, GU9 7SW. Tel 0252 710994.

Institute of Management Services, 1 Cecil Court, London Road, Enfield, Middlesex, EN2 6DD. Tel 081 363 7452.

Insulation and Environmental Training Agency, Block 2, Unit 203/4, Cannock Chase Enterprise Centre, Walkers Rise, Hednesford, Staffordshire, WS12 5QU. Tel 0543 871337.

Insurance Industry Training Council, 271a High Street, Orpington, Kent, BR6 0NW. Tel 0689 896711.

International Trade and Services Industry LB, Institute of Chartered Shipbrokers, 3 Grace Church Street, London, EC3V 0AT. Tel 071 626 3058.

Joint Industry Council for Lift Truck Operating, Scammell House, High Street, Ascot, Berkshire, SL5 7JF. Tel 0344 23800.

Joint National Horse Education and Training Council, The Stables, Rossington Hall, Great North Road, Doncaster, South Yorkshire, DN11 0HN. Tel 0302 864242.

Knitting and Lace Industries Training Resources Agency, 7 Gregory Boulevard, Nottingham, NG7 6LB. Tel 0602 605330.

Languages Lead Body, 20 Bedfordbury, London, WC2N 4LB. Tel 071 379 5134.

Law Society, Professional Standards & Development Directorate, Ipsley Court, Barrington Close, Redditch, Worcestershire, B98 0TD. Tel 071 242 1222.

Leathergoods Industry Training Organisation, Walsall Chamber of Commerce, St Paul's Road, Wood Green, Wednesbury, West Midlands, WS10 9QX. Tel 021 556 0959.

Library Association, 7 Ridgmount Street, London, WC1E 7AE. Tel 071 636 7543.

Local Government Management Board, Secretariat for Amenity Horticulture Lead Body, Arndale House, Arndale Centre, Luton, Bedfordshire, LU1 2TS. Tel 0582 451166.

Local Government Management Board, Housing Sector Consortium, Arndale House, Arndale Centre, Luton, Bedfordshire, LU1 2TS. Tel 0582 451166.

London Underground Ltd, 55 Broadway, London, SW1H 0BD. Tel 071 222 5600.

Management Charter Initiative, Russell Square House, 10–12 Russell Square, London, WC1B 5BZ. Tel 071 872 9000.

Man-Made Fibre Industry Training Advisory Board, Central House, Gate Lane, Sutton Coldfield, West Midlands, B73 5TS. Tel 021 355 7022.

Manufacturing & Development Director IBM (UK), W A Consultants, 17 Devon Road, Cheam, Surrey, SM2 7PE. Tel 081 661 0428.

Marine and Engineering Training Association, Rycote Place, 30–38 Cambridge Street, Aylesbury, Buckinghamshire, HP20

1RS. Tel 0296. 434943.

Marketing Services Board, 49a High Street, Yeadon, Leeds, West Yorkshire, LS19 7SP. Tel 0532 508955.

Meat Industry Training Organisation, PO Box 661, Winterhill House, Snowdon Drive, Milton Keynes, Buckinghamshire, MK16 1BB. Tel 0908 609829.

Mechanical Engineering Services Consortium, Gear House, Saltmeadows Road, Gateshead, Tyne and Wear, NE8 3AH. Tel 091 490 1155.

Merchant Navy Training Board, 4th Floor, Weddel House, 13/14 West Smithfield, London, WC1A 9JL. Tel 071 702 1100.

Mining Industry Lead Body, c/o Education & Training Branch, Eastwood Coal, Eastwood Hall, Mansfield Road, Eastwood, Nottingham, NG16 3EB. Tel 0773 532111.

Motor Industry Training Standards Council, 201 Gt Portland Street, London, W1N 6AB. Tel 071 436 6373.

Museum Training Institute, Kershaw House, 55 Well Street, Bradford, West Yorkshire, BD1 5PS. Tel 0274 391056.

NACOSS (National Approval Council for Security Systems), Queensgate House, 14 Cookham Road, Maidenhead, Berkshire, SL6 8AJ. Tel 0628 37512.

National Association of Chimney Sweeps, St Mary's Chambers, 19 Station Road, Stone, Staffordshire, ST15 8JP. Tel 0785 811732.

National Association of Industrial Distributors, 74 Chester Road, Castle Bromwich, Birmingham, B36 9BU. Tel 021 776 7474.

National Association of Master Bakers, Confectioners and Caterers, 21 Baldock Street, Ware, Hertfordshire, SH12 9DH. Tel 0920 468061.

National Association of Paper Merchants, Hamilton Court, Gogmore Lane, Chertsey, Surrey, KT16 9AP. Tel 0932 569797.

National Council for Industry Training Organisations, 5 George Lane, Royston, Hertfordshire, SG8 5AR. Tel 0763 247285.

National Fencing Training Authority, Suite 18, IMEX Business

Park, Shobnall Road, Burton-on-Trent, Staffordshire, DE14 2AU. Tel 0283 512611.

National Health Service Training Directorate, St Bartholomew's Court, 18 Christmas Street, Bristol, BS1 5BT. Tel 0272 291029.

National Institute of Fresh Produce, 440 Market Towers, 1 Nine Elms Lane, London, SW8 5NN. Tel 071 720 4465.

National Joint Working Group for the Jewellery and Allied Industries, British Jewellers Association, 10 Vyse Street, Birmingham, B18 6LT. Tel 021 236 3393.

National Retail Training Council, 4th Floor, Bedford House, 69–79 Fulham High Street, London, SW6 3JW. Tel 071 371 5021.

National Textile Training Group, c/o KLITRA, 7 Gregory Boulevard, Nottingham, NG7 6LD. Tel 0602 605330.

National Wholesale Training Council, Imex House, 40 Princess Street, Manchester, M1 6DE. Tel 061 237 9199.

The Newspaper Publisher's Association, 34 Southwark Bridge Road, London, SE1 9EU. Tel, 071 928 6928.

Newspaper Society, Bloomsbury House, Bloomsbury Square, 74–77 Great Russell Street, London, WC1B 3OA. Tel 071 636 7014

Occupational Health & Safety Scottish and Vocational Qualifications Lead Body, Health & Safety Executive, Baynards House, Chepstow Place, London, W2 4TF. Tel 071 243 6000.

OPITO (Offshore Petroleum Industry Training Organisation), Forties Road, Montrose, Angus, Scotland, DD10 9ET. Tel 0674 72230.

Paintmakers Association of Great Britain, 6th Floor, Alembic House, 93 Albert Embankment, London, SE1 7TY. Tel 071 582 1185.

Pensions Management Institute, PMI House, 4–10 Artillery Lane, London, E1 7LS. Tel 071 247 1452.

Periodicals Training Council, Imperial House, 15–19 Kingsway, London, WC2B 6UN. Tel 071 836 8798.

Personnel Lead Body Secretariat, c/o Institute of Personnel

Management, IPM House, 35 Camp Road, Wimbledon, London, SW19 4UX. Tel 081 946 9100.

Petroleum Employers' Skill Council, Suite 1, Morley House, 314–322 Regent Street, London, W1R 5AB. Tel 071 255 2335.

Post Office, Management College, Coton House, Rugby, Warwickshire, CV23 0AA. Tel 0788 574111.

Precast Concrete Industry Training Association, 7th Floor, 60 Charles Street, Leicester, LE1 1FB. Tel 0533 512442.

Prison Services Lead Body, 15 Delacourt Road, London, SE3 8XA. Tel 081 305 1027.

Purchasing & Supply Lead Body, Institute of Purchasing & Supply, Easton House, Easton on the Hill, Stamford, Lincolnshire, PE9 3NZ. Tel 0780 56777.

Quarry Products Training Council, Sterling House, 20 Station Road, Gerrards Cross, Buckinghamshire, SL9 8HT. Tel 0753 891808.

Railway Industry Lead Body, British Railways Board, Tournament House, Paddington Station, London, W2 1HQ. Tel 071 928 5151.

Refractories Clay Pipes and Allied Industry Training Council, c/o University of Sheffield, School of Materials, The Robert Hadfield Building, Mappin Street, Sheffield, S1 3JD. Tel 0742 768555.

Refrigeration Industry Board, Kelvin House, 76 Mill Lane, Carshalton, Surrey, SM5 2JR. Tel 081 647 7033.

Road Haulage Industry Training Standards Council, Capitol House, Empire Way, Wembley, Middlesex, HA9 0NG. Tel 081 900 2746.

Royal Mail, Royal Mail House, 148/166 Old Street, London, EC1V 9HQ. Tel 071 250 2528.

Rural Development Commission, 141 Castle Street, Salisbury, Wiltshire, SP1 3TB. Tel 0722 336255.

Saddlers Company, Clerk to the Company, Saddlers Hall, 40 Gutter Lane, London, EC2V 6BR. Tel 071 726 8661.

Scottish Association of Master Bakers, Atholl House, 4

Torpichen Street, Edinburgh, EH3 8JQ. Tel 031 229 1401.

Scottish Distributive Industries Training Council, Alpha Centre, Stirling University, Innovation Park, Stirling, FK9 4NF. Tel 0786 451661.

Scottish Federation of Meat Traders, Perth Livestock Market, 8 Needless Road, Perth, PH2 0JW. Tel 0738 32984.

Scottish Health Service, Common Services Agency, Crewe Road South, Edinburgh, EH4, 2FL. Tel 031 332 2335.

Scottish Print Employers Federation, 48 Palmerston Place, Edinburgh, EH12 5DE. Tel 031 220 4353.

Scottish Textile Association, 45 Moray Place, Edinburgh, EH3 6EQ. Tel 031 225 3149.

Screen Printing Association (UK) Ltd, 7a West Street, Reigate, Surrey, RH2 9BL. Tel 0737 240792.

Sea Fish Industry Authority, Industrial Development Unit, Sea Fish House, St Andrew's Dock, Hull, Humberside, HU3 4QE. Tel 0482 27837.

Security Industry Training Organisation, Security House, Barbourne Road, Worcester, WR1 1RS. Tel 0905 21464.

Security Services Lead Body, IPSA, 3 Dendy Road, Paignton, Devon, TQ4 5DB. Tel 0803 554849.

Self Employed and Small Businesses Ltd, 140 Lower Marsh, Westminster Bridge, London, SE1 7AE. Tel 071 928 9272.

Ship Safe Training Group, 11–13 Canal Road, Rochester, Kent, ME2 4DS. Tel 0634 725392.

Shoe Repair Industry Training Organisation Ltd, 76 The Parade, Sutton Coldfield, West Midlands, B72 1PD. Tel 021 355 2033.

Silica and Moulding Sands Association, 19 Warwick Street, Rugby, Warwickshire, CV21 3DH. Tel 0788 573041.

SkillSet, Channel 4, 60 Charlotte Street, London, WP1 2AX. Tel 071 927 8487/8585.

Soap and Detergent Industry Association, PO Box 9, Hayes Gate House, Hayes, Middlesex, UB4 0JD. Tel 081 572 7992.

Society of British Printing Ink Manufacturers Ltd, Paintmakers Association, Alembic House, 93 Albert Embankment, London, SE1 7TY. Tel 071 582 1185.

Society of Master Saddlers, Kettles Farm, Mickfield, Stowmarket, Suffolk, IP14 6BY. Tel 0449 711642.

Standing Conference for Engineering Manufacture, The Institute of Electrical Engineers, SCEM, Savoy Place, London, WC2R 0EL. Tel 071 240 1871.

Steel Training Ltd, Staybright Works, Weedon Street, Sheffield, S9 2FU. Tel 0742 446833/448088.

Sugar Industry Association, British Sugar Plc, PO Box 26, Oundle Road, Peterborough, PE2 9QU. Tel 0733 63171.

Synthetic Sports Surfaces Training Organisation, PO Box 91, Leicester, LE4 4EJ. Tel 0533 677588.

Telecommunications Industry Association, 20 Drakes Mews, Crownhill, Milton Keynes, Buckinghamshire, MK8 0ER. Tel 0908 265090.

Telecommunications Vocational Standards Council, 1st Floor, Dacon House, Presley Way, Milton Keynes, Buckinghamshire, MK8 0HD. Tel 0908 265500.

Timber Trade Federation, Clareville House, 26–27 Oxendon Street, London, SW1Y 4EL. Tel 071 839 1891.

Tobacco Industry Training Organisation, Glen House, Stag Place, London, SW1E 5AG. Tel 071 828 2803.

Training and Development Lead Body Secretariat, c/o NCITO, 5 George Lane, Royston, Hertfordshire, SG8 5AR. Tel 0763 247285.

Training & Education Association, Residential Estate, The Avenue, Brampford, Speke, Nr Exeter, Devon, EX5 5DW. Tel 0392 841194.

UK AEA Technology (UK Atomic Energy Authority), Rex House, 4–12 Regent Street, London, SW1Y 4PE. Tel 071 389 6591.

UK Agricultural Supply Trade Association, 3 Whitehall Court, London, SW1A 2EQ. Tel 071 930 3611.

UK Association of Frozen Food Producers, 1 Green Street, London, W1Y 3RG. Tel 071 629 0655.

UK Softwood Sawmillers Association, Silverbanks Sawmills, Banchory, Kincardineshire, AB3 3PY. Tel 0330 23366/7.

Wallcovering Manufacturers' Association of Great Britain,

Alembic House, 93 Albert Embankment, London, SE1 7TY. Tel 071 582 1185.

Warehouse Industry Training Organisation, Walter House, 418–422 Strand, London, WC2R 0PT. Tel 071 836 5522.

Waste Management Industry Training and Advisory Board, 9 Saxon Court, St Peters Gardens, Northampton, NN1 1SX. Tel 0604 20426.

Water Services Association of England and Wales, 1 Queen Anne's Gate, London, SW1H 9BT. Tel 071 222 8111.

Wire and Wire Rope Employers Association, 6 Brome Way, Spital, Wirral, Merseyside, L63 9ND. Tel 051 346 1566.

APPENDIX B

Useful Contacts

To find out more about lead body standards-development activities and those which affect you most contact:
Department of Employment, Moorfoot, Sheffield, S1 4PQ. Tel 0742 753275.

Over 60 awarding bodies are currently offering NVQs and SVQs. To learn more about the availability of NVQs contact:
The National Council for Vocational Qualifications (NCVQ), 222 Euston Road, London, NW1 2BZ. Tel 071 387 9898

To learn more about the availability of SVQs contact:
The Scottish Vocational Education Council (SCOTVEC), Hanover House, 24 Douglas Street, Glasgow, G2 7NQ. Tel 041 248 7900.

To find out which ITO(s) are relevant to your interests contact:
The National Council of Industry Training Organisations (NCITO), 5 George Lane, Royston, Hertfordshire, SG8 5AR. Tel 0763 247285.

If you are unclear which TEC serves your area contact:
TEC Support Unit, Department of Employment, Moorfoot, Sheffield, S1 4PQ. Tel 0742 753275.

If you are unclear which LEC serves your area contact either:
Scottish Enterprise, 120 Bothwell Street, Glasgow, G2 7JP. Tel 041 248 2700.
or:
Highlands and Islands Enterprise, Bridge House, 20 Bridge Street, Inverness, IV1 1QR. Tel 0463 234171.

Chris Lloyd and Amanda Cook can be contacted at:
Transcend Technology Ltd, Oakfield Park, Bilton Road, Rugby, Warwickshire, CV22 7UH. Tel 0788 543315.

Suggestions for Further Reading

There is relatively little publicly available literature on standards of competence. Most of the material you will need is either in the hands of the lead bodies and ITOs, or otherwise unpublished in the form of limited circulation reports.

The literature which does exist comes in three main categories. What follows is not an exhaustive bibliography but an introductory reading list which should help you to broaden or deepen your knowledge further in any or all of these areas.

General commentary on national developments – this comes mainly in the form of published books, articles in personnel training and management magazines, papers in academic journals, and features in the national press:

Burke, John W (1989) *Competency based education and training,* Falmer Press, London

Fletcher, Shirley (1991) *NVQs, standards and competence: a practical guide for employers, managers and trainers,* Kogan Page, London

Isabelle, Robert (1989) *A quiet revolution in the United Kingdom: new vocational training and qualification systems based on competences,* National Library of Canada

Jessup, Gilbert (1991) *Outcomes: NVQs and the emerging model of education and training*, Falmer Press, London

McCrory, Rosemary (1992) *Understanding National Vocational Qualifications and standards: a handbook*, Parthenon, Carnforth

Saunders, Murray, Fuller, Alison and Lobley, David (1990) *Emerging issues in the utilisation of NVQs*, National Council for Vocational Qualifications, London

Unwin, Lorna (1990) *NVQs at work: a guide for employers*, Open University Press, Milton Keynes

Unwin, Lorna (1990) *Implementing NVQs: case study file*, Open University Press, Milton Keynes

Strategic reviews – these are periodically undertaken or commissioned by a variety of organisations and largely take the form of published or membership reports:

Confederation of British Industry (1989) *Towards a skills revolution*, CBI

Confederation of British Industry (1991) *Business success through competence*, CBI

Confederation of British Industry (1991) *World class targets*, CBI

Confederation of British Industry (1992) *Focus on the first line – the role of the supervisor*, CBI

Constable, Professor C J (1988) *Developing the competent manager in a UK context*, Manpower Services Commission

Dent Lee Witte Plc (1991) *National Vocational Qualifications and Scottish Vocational Qualifications: guide to the business case framework*, Department of Employment, Sheffield

Johnson, Dr Ron (1989) *Towards 1992: vocational qualifications in the member states of the European Community and moves towards an open market*, National Council for Vocational Qualifications, London

Technical – this ranges from 'how–to' books to detailed methodological papers in journals and reports commissioned by the Department of Employment, NCVQ, SCOTVEC and others:

Competence and assessment, The quarterly journal of the Department of Employment's Methods Strategy Unit, Department of Employment, Sheffield

Etherton, Tim and Houston, Tony (1991) *Equal opportunities: the role of awarding bodies*, National Council for Vocational Qualifications, London

Jessup, Gilbert (1990) *Accreditation of prior learning in the context of National Vocational Qualifications*, National Council for Vocational Qualifications, London

Johnson, Charles and Blinkhorn, Steve (1992) *Validating NVQ assessment*, Department of Employment, Sheffield

Fennell, Edward (ed.) (1991) *Development of assessable standards for national certification*, Department of Employment, Sheffield

National Council for Vocational Qualifications (1991) *Criteria for National Vocational Qualifications*, NCVQ, London

Wood, R, Blinkhorn, S F, Johnson, C E and Anderson, S (1989) *Boning, blanching and backtacking: assessing performance in the workplace*. Department of Employment, Sheffield

Index

INDEX